LEARNING TO LISTEN *A Handbook for Music*

LEARNING TO

LISTEN *A Handbook for Music*

Prepared with the Humanities Staff
of the College at the University of Chicago

By GROSVENOR COOPER

THE UNIVERSITY OF CHICAGO PRESS

CHICAGO & LONDON

THE UNIVERSITY OF CHICAGO PRESS, CHICAGO 60637
The University of Chicago Press, Ltd., London W.C. 1

00 99 98 97 96 95 94 93 92 91   12 13 14 15 16 17

ISBN: 0-226-11519-4 pbk.

PREFACE

This book has arisen gradually out of the experiences of the last several years in teaching a course known as "Humanities 1" at the University of Chicago. Through the generosity of the Fund for the Advancement of Education in helping the editor find time to prepare the book for publication, it now ventures forth into the extramural world.

Humanities 1 is an introduction to music, art, and literature, and it is required of all freshmen except those few who are excused from it by reason of success in an examination taken upon entrance. The course lasts an academic year, and work in each of the three arts is distributed throughout that year. Therefore, although only one-third of the class time is devoted to music, the student has in some sense a year's course in music; he is given music assignments even in those periods during which music is not being considered in the classroom.

Work is carried on primarily by means of discussion in small groups under the guidance of an instructor who remains the same for the work in all three arts. The four weekly hours of class discussion are supplemented each week by a lecture given to all the groups together. The student's work outside the classroom consists primarily of listening assignments (some with supervision and some without) and of short essays on some of these assignments.

The aim of the course is to center the student's attention on the individual work of art. In music, this is done as follows: first, by bringing him to reflect upon the expression and the construction of a work itself without recourse to other considerations; second, by having him think about a work in the context of the formal procedures used in it; finally, by making him aware of its stylistic context as well. The course of study is cumulative, the earlier stages being included in the later, but the repertory changes in large part from stage to stage.

During the earlier years of the course a music handbook was developed which consisted of reference materials and an exposition of the rudiments of music. Instruction in and exemplification of the kinds of analysis to be carried on in class were thereby left largely to the lectures. But lectures are evanescent, and the student has trouble returning to them for help after they are over. Also, the kind of lecture that can be given under such conditions is rather circumscribed. It was therefore decided at a later date to include in the book essays which would do the work of such lectures and free the lecturers for more individual and specialized attacks upon similar problems.

As we carry on our course, the lectures and the essays in the book do not constitute the main substance of what we do. They serve, rather, almost entirely as models for similar studies of other pieces of music. Ideally, they would entirely so serve. The book, then, is intended to be a guide in a course rather than to be itself a course. It is intended to allow the use of a great variety in repertory and a considerable flexibility in approach.

The name of only one author appears on the title page, since he was chosen as editor. But several authors other than the editor have labored over this book: the late Millard P. Binyon, Messrs. W. Scott Goldthwaite, Edgar Smith Rose, and David G. Williams, and Miss Ethel Werfel. Since the editor has cut, augmented, revised, and partly rewritten the words of all his fellow authors, they should certainly not be held responsible for any vitiating crudities or ineptitudes which may have been introduced into their otherwise excellent expositions. The editor must assume the blame for any shortcomings of the book. Indeed, as both author and editor, he is entirely responsible for the three chapters entitled "Movement," "Form," and "Style." In the preparation of these he has had the advantage of useful criticism on the part of almost all his colleagues in Humanities 1. In particular, however, he is grateful to Messrs. Harold Haydon, Knox C. Hill, and Leonard B. Meyer for detailed and helpful suggestions.

The book in its present form differs from the one that has been in use for some time chiefly in the arrangement of the text. Formerly, essays and more informational materials were each grouped together. They now appear in the order in which they are most likely to be used.

The illustrations near the end of the book include several songs and other tunes which have been found useful for class work.

GROSVENOR COOPER

TABLE OF CONTENTS

TO THE LISTENING READER

The mere reading of a book about music, no matter how careful that reading, will not suffice to lead to musical understanding. This may strike you as being a curious statement with which to begin a book designed to help you toward such an understanding, but it is true. Repeated and attentive listening to much music is the only necessary source of a feeling for it. Without repeated and attentive listening to much music, other things, such as books and lectures, can give you but a shadowy idea of what it might be like to have a direct perception of musical process.

A great deal of music has poured into the ear of everyone who reads these lines, but so has a great deal of water doubtless poured over his head in the shower. And the shower-bath method of listening to music—the method of standing in simple passivity under it, while the mind is occupied elsewhere—does no more for the listener than give him soothing impersonal companionship as he goes about his business.

"If," you may ask, "you demand attentive listening, what should I listen for?" This is a frequent and an honest question. It requires a direct answer, even though that answer can be annoying. You should attend to whatever is going on in the music; you should follow where it leads.

After you have listened to a piece as often and as directly as you can, let things about it be pointed out to you. If you have been really attentive without prejudging your capacities, you will discover those things to be part of your experience whether you had noticed them before or not. Eventually, the things which are pointed out to you will lead toward ways of experiencing music—ways which will inculcate habits of hearing.

It is a curiosity of the human mind that fear of not understanding, or of not remembering, wonderfully inhibits the understanding and the memory. You have certainly had the experience of forgetting something which you knew perfectly well but were trying too hard to remember, and then of remembering it at some more vacant moment—perhaps while putting on your shoes. The establishment of a habit is not an instantaneous process. Failures of understanding and of memory are sure to occur. One must simply know in one's heart that they will occur and believe that with practice they will occur less and less frequently. If one does not so believe, they are likely to have a manifold recurrence. In one way or another, all knowledge begins in an act of faith.

The method of teaching favored in this book is that of pointing out to the careful listener things about the music to which he has carefully listened, thus helping him to hear more directly. This method is carried out in the three chapters entitled "Movement," "Form," and "Style." These chapters contain a certain amount of information, but that information is not the main thing about them. Information is important, however. The other chapters in the book are there chiefly for the purpose of conveying information which experience has shown to be helpful, if not always entirely necessary.

Information can be learned from somebody, in or out of a book, but understanding is attained only by one's self—perhaps through somebody but not from him. Therefore you would do well to come into the closest association with music that you are capable of. Not everyone can play an instrument, but everyone can sing, hum, or whistle. Singing is best. The physical and mental feeling of singing (or playing) brings one closer to the substance of music than any amount of listening can. With personal experience as a foundation, one can learn yet more about the feel of music from watching singers and players. Do not underestimate the visual side of musical performance. Such aspects of musical feeling as phrasing or intensity, for instance, are intimate things.

We now come to a necessary evil in a book of this sort. In order to point out things about music, one must be able to locate them in the music. This can be done readily only by means of musical notation. An elementary knowledge of notation, such as to enable one to follow a score, will suffice for our purposes here.

Following a score is not the same thing as reading music. Reading music means two things: At its best, it means imagining the sound of a piece by looking at the score of that piece; on a lower level, it means the ability to play or sing from the written notes. The reading of music, in either sense, is not necessary to the reading of this book. What is more important, the reading of music is not at all necessary to musical understanding. If, when you are watching the score while listening to a piece, you know at any point in that piece what the corresponding point in the score is, you know enough about musical notation for the purposes of this book—indeed, for any but purely professional purposes. The information supplied in the first chapter, combined with a little diligent practice and sympathetic help, should enable you to acquire the appropriate skill. It should even enable you to play a bit on the piano by the hunt-and-peck system. There are a few invented examples in this book which you may want to hear independently of any outside help.

Finally, in spite of all that has been said, there is going to be a great temptation to read about the music first and listen to it afterward. Do not succumb to this temptation. One undertaking the study of music could not possibly make a greater mistake than to read about (and even talk about) a piece without first having listened to it with care. The following procedure is recommended for studying the pieces taken up in this book: First, listen to the music; then, listen to the music while watching the score; repeat these steps until you have the music well in mind. Next, read the discussion; if you do not know to which passages in the piece particular points in the discussion refer, listen and watch until you do. But always listen first and read afterward; then listen again. When all is said and done, only music can teach you music.

MUSICAL PROCESS

1. RUDIMENTS

A musical composition is basically an organization of sounds. Sounds as physical phenomena fall mainly into two classes: *tone* and *noise*. Occupying an intermediate position somewhere between tone and noise are *vocables*, the vowel and consonant sounds of speech. Tones, noises, and vocables may all serve as musical material. Nor should one overlook the very important part played in music by the absence of sound—*silence*. The sounds of certain percussion instruments (bass drum or cymbals, for example) are noises, from the physical point of view, and can be ordered rhythmically and dynamically but in no other way, whereas tones are capable of being ordered melodically and harmonically as well. Vocables, when employed musically in song, themselves become tones and so need not be separately considered here.

All sounds, irrespective of type, have their physical origin in vibratory motion of some sort. If the vibratory motion is irregular and relatively complex, the resulting sensation is called "noise." If the motion is periodic and relatively simple, the resulting sensation is called "tone." The physical properties of any tone are four in number: (1) frequency (i.e., so many vibrations per second), (2) harmonic structure, (3) amplitude of vibration, and (4) duration. Translated into their psychological equivalents, these become, respectively, *pitch*, *quality* (i.e., "tone-color" or timbre), *loudness*, and *duration*. For example, let us note the behavior of the *A*-string of a violin when that string is set in motion through the action of the bow. Since it is of a certain length, tension, diameter, and density, the string will oscillate periodically to and fro at a frequency of 440 vibrations per second.[1] These vibrations, being reinforced and given resonance by the body

1. This is but one of several "standard" pitches for *A*.

3

of the violin, are communicated to the surrounding air and thence transmitted to the ear, where they give rise to the sensation of definite pitch, in this instance the note *A*, located in the second space of the treble staff (see p. 18). The string vibrates not only as a whole, however, but also in many fractional parts, producing thereby harmonics or overtones which have to do with the quality of the tone. It is quality or timbre which enables us to identify the tone as being that of a violin and not that of a clarinet, flute, or some other instrument. If the pressure exerted on the string by the bow is increased, the string will be drawn further from its initial position of rest, and the amplitude of its vibrations will be extended. The result is an increase in loudness of tone. And, finally, like all other sounds, the note *A* produced on the violin has extension in time, that is, duration. These observations apply in essence to all musical tones, whether the sounding medium be a stretched string, an inclosed column of air, a reed, an elastic membrane, or some solid body. And in every case the attributes which qualify the tone for musical use are definite pitch and individual quality.

Obviously, music as an organized art depends for its very existence on the availability of a variety of tones, differing in pitch and quality and susceptible of variation in loudness and duration. But various voices and instruments can unite in ensemble only if they use a common vocabulary of tones. Such a vocabulary, as crystallized in musical scales, forms the pitch material of music. There are many different tonal vocabularies, just as there are many different languages, none of which is in universal use.

As we have seen, the properties of tone are pitch, quality, loudness, and duration. In musical discussions, three of these properties, namely, quality, loudness, and duration, are usually considered under the headings of *tone-color* (or timbre), *dynamics*, and *rhythm*, respectively. Using these more familiar terms, we shall now present some remarks about them, beginning with rhythm, dynamics, and pitch.

RHYTHM

A distinction must be made at the outset between the actual note lengths in a piece and the measurement of time. Let us take a particular example. Sing the beginning of the national anthem and notice this in yourself as you sing: You think of the words and music, "O say can you see by the dawn's early light," as falling into two groups, each of which is a finished unit: "O say can you see" and "by the dawn's early light." Each of these seems unfinished if you stop in the middle of it. The mind thinks of the actual notes in a piece as coming in groups. If you clap your hands each time you sing a note, you will find that these two groups are the same in rhythm—in the time pattern of claps—though not in pitch. When you talk about this kind of grouping of the various notes in their patterns of relative duration—long and short—you are talking about that which, for want of a more precise term, we commonly call simply "rhythm."

Now start clapping your hands as regularly as a clock in accordance with the rhythm of "say can you" and "dawn's early" and sing again, against this clapping. Now your regular claps act as a measure of the relative lengths of the notes in the song. "See" and "light" last for two claps, for instance. Furthermore, without especially wanting to, you have made some claps louder than others: certainly the first clap on "see" and the first on "light"; perhaps the one on "say" and the one on "dawn's." This is because your mind organizes these claps into groups of three. When you talk about this kind of grouping, you are talking about what we call "meter."

If, now, you sing the same thing faster (or slower) than before, while still clapping out the meter, you will discover that the "clock" of your claps is going faster (or slower); the resulting sensation of relative speed should be referred to as "tempo."

By an unfortunate imprecision of terminology, the meaning of the word "rhythm" commonly includes the meanings of the words "meter" and "tempo"; but "rhythm" also means everything about sensations of time in music other than meter and tempo. You are strongly advised to restrict your use of the word "rhythm" to the latter meaning, so that your thinking about music may be more precise. Your words, then, are *rhythm*, *meter*, and *tempo*.

Let us now translate "clap" into the more formal "pulse." Musical time is measured by pulses which are thought of as regular, though they may not be so regular as the ticks of a clock. These pulses are called *beats*.

Beats tend to fall into groups of two or three. These groups provide the basis for dividing musical time into the commonest *measures* or *meters*. Individual pulses are thought of as being divisible into halves or thirds, fourths or sixths, and so on; and groups of pulses (two's or three's) are thought of as being themselves capable of being grouped in two's or three's. For instance, there may be six beats to a measure in three groups of two pulses or the same number of beats in two groups of three pulses; there may be four beats to a measure, each beat being divided in halves, or there may be four beats, each beat being divided in thirds. And measures themselves are grouped, as we shall see later.

Metrical groupings are affected by tempo. It is possible for the tempo to be so slow that one groups primarily in divisions of beats or so fast that one groups primarily in numbers of measures (for instance, in a fast waltz).

NOTATION

The information in this section is not needed for an understanding of the chapter. If you find yourself being puzzled rather than enlightened, skip to page 11.

In modern musical notation (which is the only kind we are considering here), in order to aid the eye, measures are separated each from the next by *bar-lines*. Measures are frequently called *bars*.

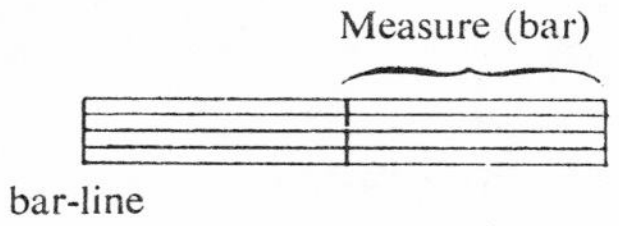

Placed at the beginning of a piece of music is a *time signature* which indicates the meter; it consists of one number placed above another, e.g., $\genfrac{}{}{0pt}{}{4}{4}$, $\genfrac{}{}{0pt}{}{3}{4}$, $\genfrac{}{}{0pt}{}{6}{8}$. A time signature is not a fraction. The upper number indicates how many beats are to be in each measure; the lower number indicates what note value is to receive one beat.

The *relative* duration in time of a musical tone, its *note value*, is indicated by the shape or appearance of the written note. Each note value has a corresponding *rest*, to indicate the measurement of silence.

𝅝 = whole-note	𝄻 = whole-rest
𝅗𝅥 = half-note	𝄼 = half-rest
♩ = quarter-note	𝄽 = quarter-rest
♪ = eighth-note	𝄾 = eighth-rest
𝅘𝅥𝅯 = sixteenth-note	𝄿 = sixteenth-rest

Given the whole-note 𝅝: when a *stem* is added to it, 𝅗𝅥, it becomes a half-note with only one-half the duration value of the whole-note. (A stem may be placed to the right of the note pointing upward, 𝅗𝅥, or to the left of the note pointing downward, 𝅗𝅥; in both cases the duration value of the note is the same.) When the half-note is filled in, ♩, it becomes a quarter-note with only one-half the duration value of the half-note. When a flag is added to the quarter-note, ♪, it becomes an eighth-note with one-half the duration value of the quarter-note. When another flag is added to the eighth-note, ♬, it becomes a sixteenth-note with one-half the duration value of the eighth-note. The subdividing process can be continued further by the addition of more flags. (When single eighth-notes or sixteenth-notes are written, the flags are curved, ♪; when a group of them occurs, however, they are joined by straight flags, ♫♫.)Therefore, if a whole-note, o, is held for 4 beats, a half-note, ♩, is held for 2 beats; a quarter-note, ♩, is held for 1 beat; an eighth-note, ♪, is held for ½ beat; and a sixteenth-note, ♬, is held for ¼ beat. A whole-rest, ▬, indicates silence for 4 beats; a half-rest, ▬, indicates silence for 2 beats; a quarter-rest, ⳡ, indicates silence for 1 beat; an eighth-rest, ⵌ, indicates silence for ½ beat; and a sixteenth-rest, ⵌ, indicates silence for ¼ beat.

Not every relative duration can be indicated by this system; therefore three accessory devices are necessary:

1. The *dot*.—A dot placed to the right of a note or rest indicates that its value is to be increased by one-half. Thus ♩. = the value of 2+(½ of 2), or 3 quarter-notes. Another dot halves the value of the dot which precedes it, and so on. Thus ♩.. = the value of ♩+♩+♪+♬.

2. The *tie*.—A tie is a curved line connecting two successive notes of the same pitch; it indicates that the second note is simply to be held as a continuation of the first. The previous value (♩..) could be expressed thus: ♩ ♩ ♪ ♬. A tie is often used to indicate a value which lasts over the bar-line. For example, ♩ ♩ has the value of ♩.

3. *Written-in numbers*.—Such numbers are used for two purposes: to indicate a temporary change from the established grouping (e.g.,

has the value of two quarter-notes, and the group of three notes must be performed in the same amount of time it took to perform the previous two) and to indicate some subdivision not otherwise allowed for in the system (e.g.,

One other device needs mention here: a *fermata* (or *hold*) ⌢ placed over a note or rest indicates that it is to be held indefinitely beyond its normal length. Here is an example to illustrate meter and note values:

The ¾ indicates that there are to be 3 beats in each measure and that each quarter-note is to receive 1 beat. There will then be either three quarter-notes in each measure or any other combination of note values the sum of which will equal three quarter-notes. Each one of the above measures contains 3 beats.

The commonest meters (others occur on occasion) are these:

Simple meters.—Those in which the fundamental pulses subdivide into groups of two, four, eight, etc.:

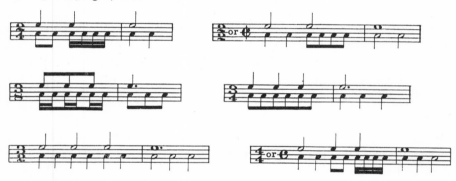

Compound meters.—Those in which the fundamental pulses subdivide into groups of three, six, twelve, etc.:

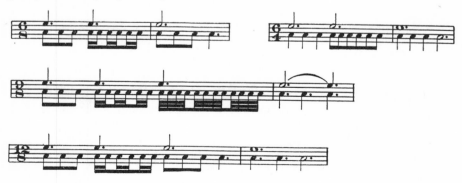

(In compound meters the upper number in the time signature is always a multiple of three.)

Change of meter may be indicated by changing the time signature, e.g.,

Occasionally, this necessitates indicating the relationship between the note values of the adjacent meters, e.g.,

In the first case, each measure in the new meter must occupy the same amount of time as did each in the old. In the second case, the quarter-note pulse must remain unvaried, and the measures in the new meter are longer than those in the old.

A composer may write a double meter to indicate that two meters are combined ("polymeter") or that there is constant change from one to the other and back, or both, e.g.,

Or, especially for transitory effects of change, stress marks (>), and, perhaps, a regrouping of flags, may be employed to insure a performance that will allow the ear to perceive the groupings, e.g.,

This is the same as

It must be remembered that the note values described above indicate only the relative duration of tones: for example, they indicate that a whole-note is to be held twice as long as a half-note, that a half-note is to be held twice as long as a quarter-note, etc. But precisely how many seconds any given note value is to be held is not indicated by the note values themselves. It is indicated by *tempo* markings.

The most accurate indication of the tempo desired by the composer is achieved by means of *metronome markings* before a piece. (A metronome is a mechanical instrument which can be regulated to tick evenly at any desired speed.)

The indication ♩ = M.M. 100 means that 100 quarter-notes are to be played per minute (or that each quarter-note is to last $\frac{1}{100}$ of a minute). (The M.M. means Mälzel's Metronome, patented in 1816, the instrument being named after its inventor.)

Composers more frequently, however, use less precise tempo markings, Italian words which give a general indication of the tempo and a more adequate indication of the mood or spirit of the composition. (During the last few decades composers of countries other than Italy have tended more and more to use their native languages for this purpose.) Here are the commonest ones

> *Grave:* grave, solemn, slow
> *Largo:* slow, broad
> *Adagio:* slow
> *Andante:* moving along at an easygoing pace
> *Andantino:* somewhat faster than andante
> *Moderato:* at a moderate tempo
> *Allegretto:* at a pace between moderato and allegro
> *Allegro:* quick, lively
> *Presto:* very fast
> *Prestissimo:* as fast as possible within the context

A more precise indication of tempo can be achieved by qualifying these terms. For example, the general term *allegro* is often followed by one or more modifiers. Some of the modifiers most commonly used are:

> *Assai:* very
> *Con moto:* with motion
> *Molto:* much
> *Giusto:* in exact tempo
> *Ma non troppo:* but not too much
> *Moderato:* moderately
> *Vivace:* with vivacity

Other qualifying words indicate the style of playing or the feeling to be suggested. The words used for this purpose are legion, and no list would be likely to be helpful.

Gradual changes of tempo are indicated thus:

Accelerando: gradually becoming faster

Ritardando or *rallentando:* gradually becoming slower

Tempo rubato: flexibility of tempo consisting of slight accelerandos and ritardandos which alternate according to the requirements of the musical expression

DYNAMICS

Relative loudness, or intensity, need not detain us long. Not only are *dynamic marks* used in the notation of music (in order to indicate the relative loudness or softness of tone), but also—and very frequently—the Italian words of which they are abbreviations are used in the discussion of music. The commonest ones are:

pp	= *pianissimo*	= very soft
p	= *piano*	= soft
mp	= *mezzopiano*	= medium soft (rather soft)
mf	= *mezzoforte*	= medium loud (rather loud)
f	= *forte*	= loud
ff	= *fortissimo*	= very loud
≤	= *crescendo*	= gradually becoming louder
≥	= *decrescendo* or *diminuendo*	= gradually becoming softer
sf	= *sforzato* or *sforzando*	= sudden stress on a single note or chord
fp	= *forte-piano*	= loud followed by soft
pf	= *piano-forte*	= soft followed by loud

PITCH

When two tones differ in pitch, we say that one is "higher" or "lower" than the other. One person is said to have a high-pitched voice, another a low-pitched voice. In a keyboard instrument such as the piano, the keys at the performer's right will, when struck, produce relatively high notes, while those at his left will produce relatively low notes. That we think of pitch in spatial terms is evident too from our system of musical notation. In written or printed music, progression from one pitch to another is represented by change of position, up or down, of notes on a staff which extends across the page. Pitch may be said to refer, then, to the position of a tone in a series or scale running from "low" to "high." A peculiarity of this series is that not all members of it are felt to be completely different from all other members. Any given pitch seems to be reduplicated by certain higher and lower pitches. The feeling that the large scale running from low to high is really a small scale which is repeated at higher and higher pitches is the phenomenon of the octave. (When men and women sing the same tune together, they usually sing in octaves.)

The extreme high and low pitches in any given voice or instrument, or in any given melody, define its *range*. Any section of this range is called a "register." For instance, the national anthem has a range larger than that of most voices; at its top it exceeds the upper register and at its bottom the lower register of most voices. The words *treble* and *bass* are general terms for, respectively, the highest and lowest pitches going on at any one time in a piece.

Pitch is *physically* determined by frequency of vibration, i.e., by the rapidity with which the vibrations of a sounding body succeed one another. What relation is there, we may ask, between high or low pitch, on the one hand, and frequency, on the other? The quicker the succession of vibrations, the higher the pitch; the slower the succession of vibrations, the lower the pitch. Or, since frequency is always given in numerical form as so many vibrations per second (e.g., 256 for middle C), the relation may be stated more exactly as: The larger the number of vibrations per second, the higher the pitch, and, obversely, the smaller the number, the lower the pitch. The frequency range of the average piano extends from about 30 complete vibrations per second for the lowest A to over 4,000 complete vibrations for the highest C. This also is the approximate range of the symphony orchestra, from the lowest note of the contra-bassoon to the highest note of the piccolo. (By a complete vibration is meant one to-and-fro movement; the terms "cycle" and "double vibration" are used in the same sense.)

The human voice, the trombone, and many stringed instruments are capable of producing tones of any desired (or undesired) pitch within their respective ranges. If the singer or instrumentalist so chooses, he can imitate the wail of a siren, which glides through all the pitches within its range. That ordinarily he does not so choose is apparent to anyone who has listened to the music of these instruments. The slide-trombone player who takes the name of his instrument too literally, or a violinist or singer who persists in an exaggerated gliding from one pitch to the next, indulges in the kind of sentimentality for which there is a derogatory German word—*Schmalz*. One of the tests of competence in singing and playing is sounding notes "in tune," at their true pitch. Such expressions as "the choir is going flat," or "the instrument is a little sharp," imply deviations from a standard. Practically all wind instruments except the slide trombone are limited by their mechanism to a definite number of tones, though by improper "lipping" the unskilful player may sound notes "out of tune." In playing a harp or any keyboard instrument, there can be no question either of gliding between pitches or of faulty intonation if the instrument has been properly tuned beforehand. It follows, then, that the pitch material of music does not form a sound continuum, like the wail of a siren, but consists of a number of pitches which can be arranged as steps—*scale* in Latin means "ladder"—running from "low" to "high"; and the task of the performing musician is to land on the right step, at the right time, and in the right way.

The total range of the pitch material of music is bounded by the lower limit of audibility but not by the upper limit. This is so despite the fact that ears differ greatly in their ability to hear extreme sounds. The tone sounded by the great 32-foot pipe of an organ (16 vibrations per second) is probably not heard as having definite pitch by most people; nor is it likely that many persons would be seriously disturbed if a pianist, aiming at the "lowest" key of the piano (around 30 vibrations per second) should by mistake strike the one next to it. Vibrations at the extreme lower limit of the musical range do not fuse into single sensations of tone but are heard as a series of throbs. On the other hand, the highest *C* of the piano (over 4,000 vibrations per second), which is approximately the upper limit of the musical range, is by no means the highest audible sound. The threshold of silence is reached by many people at a point somewhere around two octaves above this, while increasingly higher frequencies are left to the ears of a dwindling number of exceptional human beings and to some animals and insects. At either extreme of the musical scale the human ear does not readily recognize pitch, and hence psychophysiology may be said to determine the tonal boundaries of music. To be of musical use, vibrations must be neither too slow in succession nor too rapid, neither so weak as to be inaudible nor so forceful as to give pain. And within these various limits, the tonal material of music disposes itself in a definite series of tones, limited in number and fixed in pitch. This is necessarily so if the composer is to work with manageable materials and if the listener is not to lose himself in bewildering complexity.

Because pianos are commonly accessible, the following remarks are illustrated by means of the piano keyboard.

The first seven letters of the alphabet (*A–G*) are used as names of different pitches within one octave, and each white key on the keyboard has a letter name or pitch name.

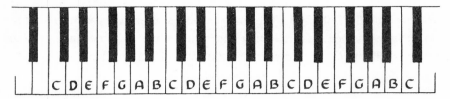

A glance at the piano keyboard shows a recurring pattern of black keys, consisting of alternating groups of two's and three's. The name of each white key can be remembered by that key's position relative to the black-key pattern; the white key immediately to the *left* of the group of *two* black ones is always *C;* similarly, the white key immediately to the *left* of the group of *three* black ones is always *F*. The distance between any one key and its nearest neighbor (whether white or black) on either side is called a *half-step*. Two half-steps make a *whole-step* (or, simply, a *step*). If one moves farther than a step, the resulting distance between pitches is called a *skip*. (The national anthem is full of skips.)

We have seen that the art of music is based on a selection of tones from among the infinite number theoretically available. We are not to infer from this that any one selection of tones is the universal basis of music but rather that the pitch vocabulary of music, of whatever place and in whatever time, is necessarily limited to a comparatively small number of tones. The musical vocabulary with which we are particularly concerned is that of Western music (European and American) of the last few centuries. If we were to examine almost any work composed within the last few centuries, we should find it to be an organization of tones which, if arranged in a stepwise series, would form either the *chromatic scale* (all the notes available in any one octave on the piano) or a selection of notes therefrom.

You are already familiar with the names of the white keys on the keyboard. Each black key, however, also has a name, which is derived from its relationship to the two white keys on either side of it.

It has been remarked above that as piano keys progress to the right, they ascend in pitch. Thus, considered in relation to the white key *C*, the black key to its *right* is *higher* (by one half-step) than *C;* it is called *C*-sharp (*C♯*).

If, however, that same black key is considered in relation to its other neighboring white key, *D*, it is called *D*-flat (*D*♭), for it is to the *left* of (or one half-step *lower* in pitch than) *D*.

We find, then, that each black key on the keyboard has two common names, depending on which of its two white-key neighbors it is being related to at the moment; it is always higher by one half-step than the white key to its left and lower by one half-step than the one to its right.

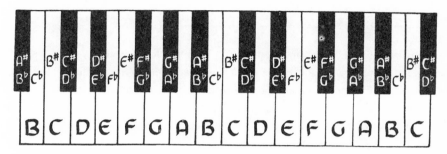

It is to be noted that between some white keys on the keyboard there are no black keys—i.e., *E* and *F*, *B* and *C*. In these cases the two white keys are one half-step apart, and so if *C*♭, for instance, were desired, the key pressed on the keyboard would be *B*; similarly, *E*♯ would be played as *F*.

Double sharps (✕) and double flats (♭♭) are used also. They indicate that a pitch is to be raised or lowered not one half-step, but two. Thus, in playing *F*✕, one would press the same white key as one would in playing *G*; in playing *D*♭♭, the same one as in playing *C*.

Pitches which sound alike on the piano but bear different names are called *enharmonic* tones. Though to the pianist *F*✕ is the same as *G*, and *A*♯ is the same as *B*♭, to a singer or violinist the two tones are not the same. A true *A*♯ is a perceptible fraction of a tone higher than *B*♭; a true *E*♭ is a fraction of a tone lower than *D*♯. Therefore, when singing or playing without piano accompaniment, the singer or violinist will raise his sharps and lower his flats more than when being accompanied by the piano, the tuning of which is "tempered"—that is, makes compromises among the various true pitches by dividing the octave into twelve equal intervals.

All sharps, flats, double sharps, and double flats are called *chromatics*. They allow the introduction of half-steps at any point in the range of pitches. The tones of the chromatic scale are close enough together so that progression from any given tone to the next above or below is felt as a step and not as a skip; they are spaced widely enough so that the average ear can easily distinguish one from another. Because of the octave interval, "the basic miracle of music," the entire musical range divides itself up naturally into octave segments, each segment of the range being like any other in the internal arrangement of its tones. Any scale is defined, then, in terms of how it divides the octave. For example, the C-major scale consists of the following tones:

$$C \quad D \quad E \quad F \quad G \quad A \quad B \quad C$$

These tones are the repertory of pitches which would be used as the basis for a passage in C major. The more the passage is restricted to these pitches, the more *diatonic* it is; the more chromatics are introduced, the more *chromatic* it is.

A *diatonic scale* consists of seven different tones within the octave and uses both whole-steps and half-steps. A diatonic scale can be divided into two halves, called *tetrachords:*

$$\overline{C \ D \ E \ F} \quad \overline{G \ A \ B \ C}$$

The various arrangements of half-steps and whole-steps (semitones and whole-tones) make the different diatonic scales which are known as *modes.*

The *major and minor modes* are the two modes of the diatonic scale most widely used in Western music between about 1600 and about 1900.

Major:

$$\overline{C \ D \ E \ F} \quad \overline{G \ A \ B \ C}$$
$$1 \quad 1 \quad \tfrac{1}{2} \quad 1 \quad 1 \quad 1 \ \tfrac{1}{2}$$

Minor:

$$\overline{C \ D \ E\flat \ F} \quad \overline{G \ A\flat \ B \ C}$$
$$1 \quad \tfrac{1}{2} \quad 1 \quad 1 \quad \tfrac{1}{2} \quad 1\tfrac{1}{2} \ \tfrac{1}{2}$$

You are advised to try out these modes at the keyboard.

The words *key* and *tonality* are used interchangeably. When we say that a piece is written in the key or tonality of C, we mean that in this composition all the notes tend toward the tone *C* as the final note. *C* is then the tonal center or *tonic* of this piece, the point from which the music departs and to which it tends to return. The scale (or scales) used in this composition will begin and end on *C*. (It is possible to use more than one mode of the same key during the course of a passage in that key.)

The degrees of the scale in the major and minor modes are referred to either by number or by special name, as follows:

Degree	Name
First	Tonic
Second	Supertonic (above the tonic; if flatted, it is called the "Neapolitan" second)
Third	Mediant (midway between tonic and dominant)
Fourth	Subdominant (the underdominant: i.e., as far below the tonic as the dominant is above it)
Fifth	Dominant
Sixth	Submediant (midway between subdominant and tonic)
Seventh	Leading tone (tone that leads to—tends to be followed by—the tonic, if it is a half-step below the tonic; if it is a whole-step below, it is simply called the seventh degree)

For example, in C (major or minor), the fifth degree (*G*) is the dominant.

We have seen that a major scale, by definition, is composed of two tetrachords, each containing a pattern of whole-step, whole-step, half-step. This pattern may be constructed starting on any pitch whatever. Only one peculiarity of nomenclature is mandatory in constructing a major scale: each letter of the alphabet (from *A* through *G*) must be used once, and once only. For instance, if you try starting on *E*, you should get *E F♯ G♯ A B C♯ D♯ E*. If you call any of the black notes flats, you will go astray.

In like manner, a minor scale can be constructed on any pitch. Any pitch can be a tonic.

NOTATION

This section (to p. 22) may be omitted.

Modern pitch notation is based upon the use of the *staff* and the *clef*.

The *staff* is the series of five parallel horizontal lines on the lines and spaces of which notes are written. Each line and each space indicates a different pitch; the lines are numbered from the bottom up. Let us suppose the third line to be *C*, for example, and the lines and spaces will represent pitches as follows:

To establish what particular pitch each line and space represents, a clef is placed on the staff at the beginning of each line of music.

The *treble* or *G* clef  establishes that the *G* above middle *C* will be situated on that line of the staff encircled by its lower loop (the second line). (Middle *C* is that *C* which is nearest the center of the keyboard.) Once this *G* is established, the other lines and spaces are named in succession: ascending on the staff is parallel with ascending in pitch (or moving to the right on the keyboard); descending on the staff is parallel with descending in pitch (or moving to the left on the keyboard).

G   A   B   C   D   E   F   G   G   F   E   D

The *bass* or *F* clef establishes that the line of the staff placed between the two dots (the fourth line) is *F* below middle *C*. Again the other lines and spaces follow in succession:

G   A   B   C   D   E   F   G   A

The *C* clef establishes that the line of the staff on which it centers is middle *C:*

C   B   A   G   F   E   C   D   E   F   G   A

The *C* clef, unlike the *G* and *F* clefs, is movable, i.e., can be placed on any line of the staff, thus making that line middle *C*. Usually it is found on the third or fourth line.

It is possible to add any number of *leger lines* above or below the staff to indicate notes of higher or lower pitch than those on the staff proper. For example, if we wanted to write the note *E* below middle *C*, using the treble (*G*) clef, several leger lines below the staff proper would be needed:

Notes off the staff proper are more difficult to read than notes on it. In practice, composers use as few leger lines as possible. *E* below middle *C* can be notated directly on the staff, in the bass clef:

Some notes, however, cannot possibly be notated on the staff proper. Composers often use the symbols *8va* ("an octave higher than written") and *8va bassa* ("an octave lower") to make notation easier.

The treble clef (*G*) is usually used for soprano voices and instruments and the right-hand part of piano music.

The alto clef (*C* third line) is used for the viola.

The tenor clef (*C* fourth line) is often used for the bassoon and the cello.

The bass clef (*F*) is used for the lower male voices and orchestral instruments and the left-hand part of most piano music.

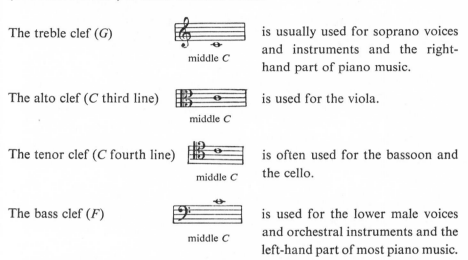

The following diagram illustrates the relative ranges of the bass, alto, and treble clefs:

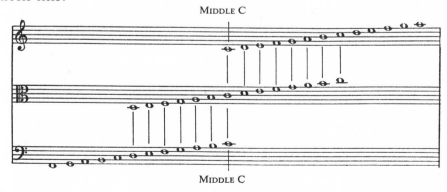

Chromatics are notated by placing the appropriate one of the following symbols before the note to which it applies:

$\sharp$ = sharp   ✕ = double sharp
$\flat$ = flat $\flat\flat$ = double flat
$\natural$ = natural (i.e., cancel any previous chromatic for this note)

We have seen that major scales other than C require chromatics. For instance (try this at the keyboard), G major requires an *F#* in order to fulfil the pattern of steps and half-steps. Therefore, instead of writing a sharp (#) each time an *F* occurs in the music, we simply write the sharp at the beginning of the piece on the *F* line of the staff (the fifth line when using the treble clef) to indicate that whenever the note *F* occurs, *F#* is to be performed instead of *F$\natural$*. This indication, at the beginning of a piece, of the sharps or flats to be observed throughout the piece is called a *key signature*.

The key signatures may be divided into sharps and flats.

SHARP KEYS

Key	Key Signature
C major	no sharps
G major	*f#*
D major	*f#, c#*
A major	*f#, c#, g#*
E major	*f#, c#, g#, d#*
B major	*f#, c#, g#, d#, a#*
F# major	*f#, c#, g#, d#, a#, e#*
C# major	*f#, c#, g#, d#, a#, e#, b#*

Note that the sharps are cumulative and that the last sharp to be added in each key is the seventh degree of the scale (the leading tone), 1 half-step below the tonic. A very simple way of recognizing the major key indicated by a signature is to look at the last accumulated sharp (the one most to the right) and count up 1 half-step; the resultant pitch is the tonic note (name of the key).

FLAT KEYS

Key	Key Signature
C major	no flats
F major	*b♭*
B♭ major	*b♭, e♭*
E♭ major	*b♭, e♭, a♭*
A♭ major	*b♭, e♭, a♭, d♭*
D♭ major	*b♭, e♭, a♭, d♭, g♭*
G♭ major	*b♭, e♭, a♭, d♭, g♭, c♭*

Note that the *next-to-the-last* flat indicates the pitch of the tonic note.

Every major key has what is called a *relative minor* key, which has the same key signature (hence "relative") but whose tonic note is situated 3 half-steps (3 letter names) below that of the major key. For example, the relative minor key of G major is 1½ steps below *G;* count down 3 half-steps from *G* (*G–F♯–F–E*) to *E*, which is then the tonic note of the relative minor scale. We find, then, that a key signature indicates either one key in the major mode or another key in the minor mode. For example:

(1)  indicates that the piece may be in either A major (the tonic note is 1 half-step above the last sharp) or its relative minor, F♯ minor (count down 1½ steps from *A*).

(2) indicates that the piece may be in either B♭ major (the tonic note is the same as the next-to-the-last flat) or its relative minor, G minor (count down 1½ steps from *B♭*).

We have said that the major and relative minor keys have identical key signatures (same sharps or flats), although they have different tonics. The scales built on the two tonics would then be, for example, the following:

B♭ major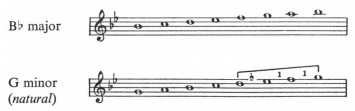

G minor (*natural*)

This minor scale, which has the same sharps or flats as the relative major scale, is called the *natural minor scale*. It is purely theoretical. In practical use there are two other minor scales, the *harmonic* and the *melodic*, both of which modify the upper tetrachord of the natural minor scale, the lower tetrachord of all the minor scales remaining identical:

G minor (*harmonic*)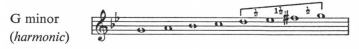

In this scale the seventh degree of the natural minor scale is raised to a *leading tone* (1 half-step below the tonic), making a distance of three half-steps between the sixth and seventh degrees.

G minor (*melodic*)

In this scale the sixth and seventh degrees of the natural minor scale are raised when ascending and lowered again when descending. (In ascending, then, the upper tetrachord is the same as that of the G-major scale; in descending, the upper tetrachord is the same as that of the natural minor scale.)

In addition, the second degree of the scale is rather often flatted. (In our example, this procedure would result in an *A♭*.)

It must be said, however, that G major and G minor (the *parallel* minor) are more closely related, having the same tonic, than are B♭ major and G minor (the *relative* minor of B♭), which have different tonics.

FOLLOWING SCORES

If you have never before followed a score, you may find these remarks of assistance:

1. A line of music on the page consists of the requisite number of staffs bound together on the left by a vertical line and sometimes also by a "brace." For instance, music for piano is written on two staffs, one for each hand, and these two staffs are grouped together by a brace, { (see p. 138). Music for string quartet is written on four staffs, one for each instrument; these four staffs may or may not be grouped together by a brace but will at least be bound by a vertical line. As a visual aid, the symbol ⋜ may be used to separate the lines of music on a page.

2. Literal repetitions are indicated, wherever possible, by :‖ = go back to the beginning and repeat up to this point; ‖: :‖ = repeat the passage between these two marks.

3. The end of a piece is always indicated by making the final bar-line double, a *double bar*. Divisions within a piece are also frequently marked off by double bars, especially if they are signalized by changes of key signature, of time signature, or of tempo.

4. Some instruments are "transposing instruments," that is, their music is written in a key or octave different from the one that it sounds in. Instruments for which the key is transposed are English horn (alto oboe), clarinet and bass

clarinet, horn, and trumpet. The reason for this is that oboes, clarinets, horns, and trumpets are made in more than one size, but the various sizes in each of the four groups are playable by the same technique (fingering and relative lip pressure). A clarinetist, for instance, is able to play all the instruments of the clarinet "family," from the highest (E♭ clarinet) to the lowest (bass clarinet), without materially altering his habits of hand and lip as he changes from one instrument to another. He considers that on the B♭ clarinet B♭ is his simplest key, and so that key is presented to him on the score in its simplest notation, i.e., as C major. Since C is one whole-tone above B♭, whatever note this clarinet is to sound is written on the score one whole-tone higher. If the note to be sounded is A, what appears on the score will be B. On the A clarinet, A is the simplest key, so that key is notated as C major. Similarly, an E♭ clarinet sounds E♭ when C is written, and the composer will write F (a tone and a half below A♭) in order to sound A♭. This kind of adjustment needs to be made for every note of a transposing instrument, the interval of transposition being the interval between the note which the instrument sounds when C is written and an actual C. On the first page of the score the C of each transposing instrument is indicated—clarinets in B♭ or E♭, horns and trumpets in E♭ or F, etc. The English horn is in F (understood).

Instruments which transpose not the key but merely the octave are the piccolo, which sounds an octave higher than the note appearing on the score, and the contra-bassoon and string bass, which sound an octave below the note on the score.

5. There are some special effects which can be produced by playing an instrument in a manner out of the ordinary. These effects must be indicated by the composer in his notation. Some of the more usual ones are listed here.

Strings:
  con sordino—with a mute on the bridge—dampens the sound
  pizzicato—pluck the strings instead of bowing
  col legno (with the wood)—tap strings with stick of bow instead of hair
  sul ponticello (on the bridge)—bow very close to the bridge—gives rather eerie
    quality
  sur la touche (on the finger board)—bow slightly over the finger board—
    vaguely flutelike ("flautando")

flageolet tones, or harmonics—upper partials of a fundamental tone—obtained by lightly touching the string instead of stopping it in the usual manner—indicated by a small circle (°) above the note

Brass:

hand-stopping (of French horn)—muting by inserting hand into the bell—changes timbre to a soft, faintly buzzing quality—indicated by a small cross (⁺) above the note

mute—pear-shaped piece of metal, wood, or cardboard inserted into bell—similar in effect to hand-stopping

cuivré—"brassy" tone achieved by increased pressure when instrument is muted

6. The manner of execution is frequently indicated in a score either by words or by special signs. The commonest of these are:

Legato ("linked") = connect the notes smoothly

Staccato ("separated") = detach the notes sharply one from another

⌒(a "slur") = for winds and voices, play or sing these notes on one breath; for strings, play these notes on one stroke of the bow; for keyboard, legato

♩ or ♩ (a dot above or below a note) = staccato

2. MOVEMENT

The only way toward a full understanding of music lies in direct attention to the continuity and organization of the tonal material itself.

If we examine the melody familiarly known as "The Londonderry Air," we can begin to see some of the principles of musical continuity and organization at work.

The melody is divided into four large sections; these are called *phrases*. As the melody is printed here one can observe some similarities among the four phrases: they are all of the same length, their rhythms are similar, and each is divided into two halves. Furthermore, all eight of these half-phrases have the same general shape: each begins with a rise and ends with a fall.

These are gross comparisons. As we listen more closely, we may notice the way the shorter notes of the melody (the eighth-notes) lead up to and away from the longer notes, which seem by contrast more weighty—more accented—though not necessarily louder. The way in which each of the half-phrases centers on these weightier notes plays a large part in our feeling for the "shape" or the "line" of the tune. The tune conveys a sense of movement toward and away from the longer notes in the middle of each half-phrase and comes to rest—at least temporary rest—at the end of each, only for the sense of movement to start afresh with the beginning of the next. This very general sense of movement is part of what we mean by the word "rhythm." But movement results not only from the relative lengths of the notes and from their accented groupings but also from the rise and fall in pitch of the tune as a whole succession of sections. Movement is not only in the rough shape—the rising and falling line—found in each half-phrase but also, and more vividly, in the relative pitches of the half-phrases and the phrases compared with one another.

The second half of the first phrase is rhythmically quite similar to the first half, but it begins by rising to a higher pitch. It is, in a sense, the same thing moved up. We feel that the whole tune—the whole line—not merely the individual tones in it—has moved; and we are led to expect now that the tune will go still higher. In other words, we have a feeling about its continuity. This is one kind of expectation in music: that motion in a certain direction (in this case, upward) will be continued until it reaches a conclusion in some way satisfying to us. Another kind of expectation in music is also illustrated by the behavior of the second phrase in relation to that of the first. The first phrase comes to a cadence (ends) on a pitch (F) which has the effect of being, so to speak, up in the air. This pitch is not one on which the whole tune could come to a satisfying conclusion. It is not the tonic. This kind of cadence is incomplete. The second phrase then begins as did the first. Now, when a phrase ending with an incomplete cadence is succeeded by another phrase that begins in the same way as did the first (or a similar way), we expect that second phrase to end on the tonic—to come to a complete cadence. The first phrase is an *antecedent;* we expect the second to be its *consequent*. This expectation is fulfilled in the second phrase of our tune. However, although we have here what are called *balanced phrases*, our expectation of continued motion upward has not yet been fulfilled. We have, then, an ambiguous feeling about these two phrases: they are balanced, and thereby cause in one sense a feeling of completion; but there is about them also a feeling of incompletion resulting from the lack of upward continuation of the melody.

The third phrase, we find, begins at a considerably higher pitch, and we now know that the general upward movement is being continued. But we notice that the second half of this phrase, although it ends differently, begins in the same way as the first half. There is a sense here of frustrated movement—of pushing against something resistant. For this reason, when, in the fourth phrase, the melody at first seems to be meeting even more resistance by "getting stuck" on one note, instead of rising, as usual, but then suddenly leaps upward to the highest tone of all, the release of energy is most satisfying—the expectation has been fulfilled, and the melody may fall to the point from which it started, for it has been where it seemed to be trying to go.

If we listen now to another well-known tune, "Adeste Fideles,"

and compare it with the "Londonderry Air," we find that "Adeste Fideles" has a quite different rhythmic quality. This is the kind of music that often causes listeners to tap their feet or nod their heads in response to the strong rhythm of the tune. One can readily imagine one's self marching to this tune. Indeed, it is a processional tune, one to be sung while marching. The sense of movement here is associated with the suggestion of bodily movement. We say that the tune has a "strong meter." The reason for this is to be found in the accentual character of the first three notes, the germ from which the rest of the tune grows rhythmically. These notes have a "foot rhythm." A foot rhythm acts

in much the same way as does a predominant foot in verse. This foot, the amphibrach (◡–◡), when repeated (◡–◡◡–◡, etc.) tends to bring about a recurrent accent in the same place in each measure. That is, the equal groups of pulses (in this case, four) constituting the measure become accentually differ-

entiated in a pattern of strong and weak. And, although the foot is obviously
not simply repeated, it establishes a rhythmic norm in the melody—a norm
against which we (unconsciously) compare other rhythms in the sequel and feel
their effects.

Although the "Londonderry Air" is metrical, its meter is not vivid: we are
more conscious of smoothly flowing eighth-notes grouped about the longer
notes than we are of any strong-weak differentiation of pulse. In "Adeste
Fideles" the four-ONE-two-three of the meter is striking.

Allied with the difference in accentual character is another prominent difference between the two tunes. We noticed that the phrase lengths in the "Londonderry Air" were the same throughout and that each phrase was divided into two
halves of equal length. The phrasing was regular or symmetrical. It moved at an
even pace. In "Adeste Fideles," the phrases are not all of the same length, nor
are the parts of the phrases. The grouping in terms of number of measures may
be diagrammed as follows (⌐⌐ means "closely linked, with only a slight feeling,
if any, of separation"):

> Phrase   I: 1+1+2   (4)
> Phrase II: 1+1+2   (4)
> Phrase III: 1+1+2   (4)
> Phrase IV: 2+2+2+2 (8)

Pointing out these variations in length is simply another way of saying that
the opening foot rhythm, or rhythmic motive, undergoes change and growth in
the melody in ways that are directly related to the rhythmic intensity of the
music.

The first two feet set up a rhythmic and melodic expectation of this sort:

But the light first note is missing at the end of bar 2. Instead, there is a group of
short notes in bar 3. While these are going on, we await the rhythm normal for
this piece (⌣–⌣). It finally arrives in bar 4. The expectation drawn out in bar 3
is sufficiently intense that most singers come down on the first note of bar 4
with a satisfied, thumping *forte*.

The second phrase begins normally, but the second foot in it is broken in the middle.

The resulting upward movement has such a strong impetus that we are barely conscious of the beginning of the next foot. This next foot is quite unlike the normal one, which has a relatively light closing note. Here we have three strongly stressed notes.

If you will imagine this cadence altered as follows:

to conform with the prevailing foot, you will see that it is distressingly out of character. The tune is positive and vigorous, not soft and gentle. At a main division, it needs a masculine ending (accented final note), not the feminine ending (unaccented final note) inherent in the amphibrach rhythm. The masculine ending here is all the more forceful for the unaccented note of the same pitch (an "anticipation") which precedes it.

The third phrase is heard in the light of the first, from which it subtly varies in rhythm:

The fourth phrase is rhythmically the most intense of all, for the foot is expanded to twice its normal length, and the phrase itself therefore becomes twice as long as any of the others. The last two feet are completely linked.

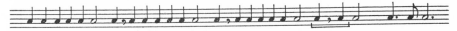

All the phrases move in a similar fashion from shorter units to longer. Each builds a rhythmic climax. Important to that climax in the last phrase is not only

the rhythm but also the way in which, in the first two feet, the long note is re-
peatedly anticipated by the short notes which precede it, making the release of
movement in the rest of the phrase all the more forceful. Also, one cannot help
comparing the third and fourth bars of the first phrase, which are there the
climax, with the third and fourth bars of the last phrase, which are here only
on the way to the climax.

Before discussing the balance of phrases, let us examine the melodic movement of the whole tune by making a skeletonized version of it, that is, by setting
forth the most emphatic notes of the melodic line. The emphasis in the tune is
on the following melodic outline:

Notice how the general movements upward and downward are contrasted and
related:

       Phrase I: up
       Phrase II: down
       Phrase III: down from highest point to lowest
       Phrase IV: up, then down—then down again—with a final emphatic movement

with a distinct break between Phrases II and III; and how the phrases are further
interrelated by means of the tones indicated by notes in parentheses. The *general*
movement, indeed, is up and down from one step of the scale to the next: it is
conjunct motion, although in the *specific* movement (the actual notes of the
tune), there is much disjunct motion (motion that skips one or more steps of
the scale).

The melodic outline makes clear how strong and how specific are one's
expectations of what the next emphatic note within a phrase is going to be.
Notice, for example, how one anticipates the C♯ in bar 3—or the E at the end
of Phrase II.

The first phrase ends with an incomplete cadence. The second phrase, however, does not become its consequent; it ends with a complete cadence, but on the

"wrong" pitch: it has modulated.[1] This cadence has, so to speak, the shadow of finality without the substance. The effect of it is to make both the first two phrases stand in need of a consequent. The third phrase, however, although it reverts to the original key, does not act like a consequent either, for it begins suddenly at a pitch new to the tune and has a melodic shape quite opposed to that of the first phrase. Furthermore, its incomplete cadence distinctly echoes the complete cadence of the second phrase. In terms of balance, the music is no farther here than it was there. The consequent has been postponed. The fourth phrase, by acting in its beginning like the first phrase and in its ending like the second—but with its complete cadence on the "right" pitch—becomes the expected consequent.

By returning, after this analysis, to the "Londonderry Air," we find that the movement of phrases is more subtle there than we had observed. We had observed that the first two phrases are antecedent and consequent, that they leave unfulfilled an expectation of upward movement, and that the last two phrases fulfil that expectation. But these last two phrases produce a rhythmic as well as a melodic climax, in much the manner of "Adeste Fideles," for they tend to coalesce into one in the pattern of lengths $2+2+4$. Furthermore, the last two bars beautifully complete the balance, for they are a condensed version, with a complete cadence, of the way in which the melody began.

Both the melodies we have been discussing are tonal, that is, they come to rest on a single pitch or tonic, and both are songs. But there are striking differences between them. The "Londonderry Air" has more symmetrical phrasing, a more even pace; its sections are roughly of the same shape; it moves quietly and steadily, but it moves quite far from a relatively low pitch to a relatively high one and back again; it has a large range and a line abounding in skips ("disjunct motion"). Its associations are lyrical, and it has a singer's climax: the most natural response to it is to sing, hum, or whistle.

"Adeste Fideles" has uneven phrasing—a dynamic pace. Its movement is more rapid and accented; within a rather small range it goes up and down the scale ("conjunct motion") in a forceful way. It can readily be sung, hummed, or whistled, but its associations are not only lyrical but also kinetic: the most natural response to it includes bodily movement.

In speaking of these two melodies, considerations of both large and small sections have entered into the discussion: motive and phrase; foot rhythm and

1. The modulation is from A (the home tonic) to E (the dominant).

phrase rhythm; movement within the phrase and movement of the phrases as wholes with respect one to another. Attention both to details and to larger sections is important, because a piece of music progresses not only from one moment to the next, so to speak, but also as a whole thing. At any one moment during the progress of the music one must remember the past and anticipate the future, for the force of musical movement—the feeling of continuity—depends upon what one anticipates the future progress of the music will be, given its past at any moment. And in order to anticipate the future, one needs not only to follow the music in detail as it moves along but also to have some feeling for its larger shape—its form.

Let us now turn to a piece longer than either of the two melodies we have so far studied: the minuet from Mozart's String Quartet in G Major, K.387.[2] If, in listening to this piece, we try to notice which are the largest divisions, we discover them to be three: the *menuetto*, the *trio*, and the repetition of the *menuetto*.[3] We may symbolize these sections as *A B A*. Although the second *A* is only half as long as the first (on account of the omission of the internal repetitions), the ear is satisfied that the first *A* has been balanced. It is the nature of what occurs in a given section of music—rather than the length of that section—which is most important in causing a feeling of balance between it and some other section.

But other divisions into sections are noticeable besides the large *A B A*. The minuet and the trio are each divided (as the repeat marks indicate) into two sections, each of which is repeated. We may symbolize these divisions as follows:

A	*B*	*A*[4]
aabb	*aabb*	*ab*

Perhaps we notice that of these smaller divisions, *b* is always longer than *a*. Upon closer listening, we discover that this is true because *b* includes as its ending a varied repetition of *a*. (Compare bars 1–40 with bars 63–93, and bars 94–118 with bars 127–147.) We may therefore go further in our diagram of divisions:

2. "K.387" means No. 387 in Köchel's catalogue; this is the standard way of identifying Mozart's works. For the score see p. 33.

3. "*Menuetto D.C.* (*da capo*) *senza replica*" means that the minuet is to be played again without observing the repeat marks.

4. In moving from one large section, such as *A*, to another, such as *B*, one starts afresh with the lower-case letters in the symbolization of the smaller sections.

A	B	A^5
a a ba' ba'	*a a ba' ba'*	*a ba'*

There would be no point in noticing these subdivisions into similar and contrasting sections were it not for the fact that they are the external evidence of the larger internal movement of the music. What, in broad outline, is the nature of this movement? We may, in part, answer this question after making a brief study of the phrases in the first large section of the minuet.

The first phrase (bars 1–10) has an incomplete cadence:

It gives rise, therefore, to the expectation that it will be complemented by a phrase like itself in material but ending with a complete cadence.

As the second phrase (bars 11–20), after a brief link, begins, we feel that, in spite of the variation

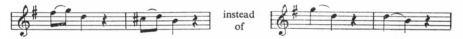

the material of the first phrase is about to be repeated, and we expect that this new phrase will be the consequent complementing the first phrase. This feeling is heightened by the continuation of the second phrase. The cadence of this phrase, however, denies the expectation of completion in two respects: it, too, is incomplete, and it is in a new key:

5. A varied repetition of an *a* is usually symbolized as *a'*; a further, differently varied repetition, as *a''*, etc.

We are left, then, in bar 20, with a feeling of incompleteness. In order to relieve this feeling, there must be in the sequel a passage which comes to an end in the original key.

The music does not proceed immediately, however, to such a passage. It stays (through bar 40) in the new key, and, instead of repeating the motives of bars 1–20, introduces two new themes—statements of two new musical ideas (bars 21–28 and 29–36)—each with its own individual motives, followed by four bars which emphasize the *relative* conclusiveness of the whole large section (bars 1–40) by a complete cadence in the new key. As a result of this procedure, the music contains a whole long antecedent section (bars 1–40) which is emphatically in need of a consequent. This need is satisfied by the music in bars 63–93, which, in effect, repeat bars 1–40 but remain in the original key. Bars 63–93 rectify, so to speak, a "mistake" made in bars 1–40. Put in another way, the expectation frustrated in bars 1–40 is fulfilled in bars 63–93. (The reader may wish to investigate for himself the similar relationship between bars 94–118 and bars 127–147 of the trio.) The antecedent section has been balanced by its consequent, but not until another, rather long, passage (bars 41–62) has intervened. About this intervening passage, suffice it for the present to point out that it delays considerably the entrance of the consequent section.

Although the relationships among the largest divisions of many pieces may be symbolized as *A B A*, this symbolization is highly generalized and says very little about the actual form of any individual piece. For example, Chopin's Prelude in F Sharp Major, op. 28, No. 13,[6] is ternary in form (*A B A*) but is quite unlike the Mozart minuet in several ways, three important ones of which are these: First, whereas there are distinct pauses between the minuet and the trio and between the trio and the da capo of the minuet, the Prelude is continuous. Second, there is no "da capo senza replica" in the Prelude, because the repeat of *A* in that piece is both varied and partial. Here is the scheme of the Prelude:

A (bars 1–20) *B* (21–28) *A*—or, if you will, *A'*—(29–36, a varied repetition of 13–20) Coda[7] (37–38, reminiscent of *B*).

Third, the Mozart piece abounds in a variety of material containing several contrasting motives and themes; the Chopin piece, on the other hand, is ex-

6. See p. 134.

7. A coda is a section added after a formal procedure has been completed.

traordinarily homogeneous: its immediate continuity of movement is striking throughout. Before going into more details about the material of the Mozart, however, let us examine the Chopin more closely.

If we ask what the nature of the motive is in the opening bars of this piece, we must say, to begin with, that there are really two motives: one in the treble and one in the bass. The treble motive consists of this melodic idea

and other tones which blend with the melody in such a way that they support it—make its sound fuller—without detracting from it: the melody is harmonized with consonant chords.[8]

In the opening bars of the piece the bass is apprehended as something different from the treble by virtue of its contrasting rhythm. The bass consists, in section *A* and its partial recurrence, of repetitions and variations of the following pattern or figure:

But the ear does not hear the bass and treble as unrelated, though simultaneous, things. Careful listening to the bass figure will reveal that most of its constituent tones are consonant with the treble. The second and third tones, however, are not; they are dissonant. Note carefully, even if several repetitions of only a few bars are necessary, the effect achieved by the dissonances with respect to the consonances which precede and follow them. Dissonance is one of the main sources of musical movement. The ear is habituated to the expectation that in this kind of music dissonance will resolve in consonance. The extraordinary tranquillity of this Prelude is heightened by its slight troubling through the bass dissonances which, with their regular—and consequently expected—recurrence and resolution, give rise to a sense of control in the listener's mind.

8. A *chord* is two or more tones sounding simultaneously. In more common usage, two different tones sounding together make a *harmonic interval* (or simply *interval*); two or more intervals sounding together (three tones, four tones, sometimes more than four) make a *chord*. A *consonance* is an interval such that the ear tends to accept it as being at rest. Consonance is relative; its opposite pole is dissonance. A *dissonance* is not at rest: the ear expects it to move to a consonance (to be "resolved"). A consonant chord, then, is one in which each tone makes a consonance with each other tone. And we say that a melody is *harmonized* when it is accompanied by chords.

Dissonance and resolution are only one example of harmonic movement; there are broader harmonic effects which, in their turn, cause the individual chords and sequences of chords—the harmony—to move.

Listen to the first four and a half bars of the Prelude. They contain only two different chords, which appear alternately:[9]

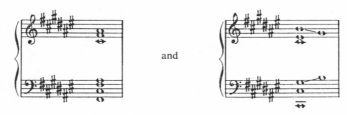

and

(All other tones in these bars make dissonances; they are "non-harmonic tones" or "non-chordal tones.") But these chords are not equally stable; the first is more at rest than the second. Notice the sense of resolution, of return to stability, in the beginning of bar 3 (or 5). The chord at the end of bar 2 (or 4) is said to have a direction—to tend to move toward, and find resolution in, another chord. Not only single chords, but a series of chords, may require resolution.

If we now turn to larger units, what is the effect of the first cadence, that in bar 7? The final chord

is the resolution, the objective, of the three chords which precede it:

9. These chords are technically known as the "tonic triad" and the "dominant seventh chord."

The cadence is complete. But there has been a modulation to the dominant (C-sharp). In itself, that is, the cadence is complete; in the piece as a whole, a sense of direction has been established by it. The piece must return to the original tonic. It does so by means of a complementary phrase—a consequent—that is, by a phrase which starts like the antecedent phrase but ends in the "home tonic" (the original key) instead of leaving it for another key. Compare this with the relationship between the second and last phrases of "Adeste Fideles."

Notice the hierarchy of harmonic movement pointed out so far: dissonance and consonance, chord progression (a sense of movement from one chord to another), and relationship between cadences.

The still larger structure of the whole Prelude (*A B A*) is *harmonically* the result of the fact that part *B* moves away immediately from the home tonic, so that a sense of completed movement cannot result merely from a repetition (in whole or in part) of *A*, but must include a return to that home tonic.

Before leaving this topic, the reader's attention is invited to the first chord in bar 13. Here, the alien note

causes the harmony to move away from the home tonic, and the return to that tonic in the cadence of bars 17–18 is made more secure by the varied repetition which follows.

The reader should now compare by ear the ending of part *B*, in bar 28, with the beginning of the piece. He will discover, if he has not already realized it, that in bar 28 the melody has reached the point from which it started. It is this peculiarity that makes it possible for a repetition of only the end of *A* to suffice for a sense of both melodic and harmonic completeness in the piece. This sense of completeness is augmented by the fact that part *B* does not contain a complete theme. It modulates and does not come to rest in the key in which it started[10] and so does not give the effect of making a statement—of setting forth a complete musical idea. The varied restatement of the end of *A* is a return to solid ground.

10. The keys are C-sharp, B, and, finally, F-sharp.

In speaking of the opening material in this piece and in describing it as a harmonized melody (a melody and accompaniment), we were describing its texture—the relationship among themselves of the strands of sound, the lines, which go on simultaneously. This texture, in comparison with that of the Mozart minuet, remains much the same throughout the piece. In the Mozart, the variety of material is complemented by a variety of texture.

This variety may be described as various degrees of tendency toward one or the other of two poles of texture, the *homophonic* and the *contrapuntal*, or *polyphonic*. The extreme of homophony would be a texture in which an accompaniment was completely subordinated to a melody. The extreme of counterpoint (or polyphony) would be a texture in which all the parts were equally melodic. (A single, unaccompanied melodic line is said to have a "monophonic" texture.)

In the Mozart minuet, the opening trochaic motive in the first violin is succeeded in each of its appearances by a single chord in the other instruments. But the next motive, the curious *pf* iambic motive which clashes with the meter (is "syncopated") and which moves upward chromatically, is treated differently. We hear this chromatic line all alone in bars 3 and 4, then in descending sequence (repeated at a lower pitch) in bars 5 and 6. Then the cello inverts it (plays it down instead of up) and the other instruments join in, making the texture fuller. The result is highly chromatic in its harmony. The second phrase goes through the same sequence of textures in a more elaborate form. Here the chromatic motive is treated in imitative counterpoint, that is, what the second violin plays in bar 13 is played by the viola in bar 14, and there is the same relationship in bars 15 and 16. At the same time, the first violin adds a new motive, also in descending sequence. But when bar 17 is reached, the texture becomes more homophonic and the harmony diatonic. The rest of this section (through bar 40) is more homophonic than contrapuntal, but there is considerable variety of accompaniment. Compare the accompaniment in bars 21–28 with that in bars 29–36, for instance. There is also a balance between chromaticism and diatonic harmony.

The next section (bars 41–62) is at first like the beginning of the piece, but inverted (going in the opposite direction). Starting in bar 43, however, a four-note motive

which grows naturally out of the trochaic motive in the previous bars is treated in imitation in all four instruments and builds up to a homophonic cadence. Part of this phrase is then repeated in descending sequence (bars 50–54). The next passage has two centers of interest: the first violin, and the other three instruments treated as a unit. At the end of this passage we find an ascending sequence treated in imitative counterpoint. The first violin leads, and the second violin and viola imitate together. The rest of the minuet (from bar 63 up to the trio) repeats, in its sequence of textures, bars 11–40, except that the first phrase (63–73) contains more imitation and sequence than did its predecessor (bars 11–20).

It is important to observe that the differences between the Mozart and the Chopin are all various aspects of a fundamental difference. The Mozart has more variety, the Chopin more homogeneity. Perhaps the most striking illustration of this difference lies in a comparison of the relationships between the parts we have symbolized as A and B in the two pieces. The trio of the minuet is in the minor mode (the minuet was in the major); it has quite novel thematic material; it is sharply set off by pauses from the minuet; and it begins with a striking monophonic passage, *forte*. The middle part of the Prelude stays in the major mode; although it has novel thematic material, that material, in its development, is made to conform so closely to that of the first part that it can lead smoothly into a repeat of only the end of that part; and the texture is as much like that of the first part as it can be and still be perceptibly different.

In the Mozart, there is variety in all the musical elements: variety in *rhythm*, in *melody*, in *harmony*, in *texture*, and in *dynamics*. In the Chopin, there are only the subtlest variations in all these elements. Were these two pieces scored for a large group of instruments such as an orchestra, with all its potential contrasts of timbre, instead of being in the relatively monochromatic media of the string quartet and the piano, we should find that the use of the remaining musical element, *tone-color*, would only bear out the fundamental difference between the pieces. Constant change of color would be just as inappropriate to the character of the Prelude as its opposite would be to the minuet. They are different kinds of music.

But one must not overlook the important similarities. In both pieces, as well as in the two melodies that we considered previously, balance of phrases and the attraction of tonality are important. But, beyond that, there are certain general principles of musical organization far more fundamental. There is music which is not tonal; there is music which does not move in clear-cut phrases; there is music without sequences and without imitation. But no music of any length can be coherent in form without the principles of *return*, of *variation* or of *development*, and of *contrast*. The return to a tonic, which we have seen in all the pieces discussed so far, is a special instance of a general principle. An *A B A* form is a special instance of return after contrast. The rhythmic expansion we noted in "Adeste Fideles" is development. Variation plays a prominent part in the Prelude in F Sharp. And so on. Put in a simple-minded way, something must happen in a piece—there must be a feeling of expansion about it, hence, variation or development; there must be variety, hence, contrast; and, since music is, of all the arts, the one furthest removed from references outside itself, its sense of completeness has to come from within—it has to be rounded off—hence, return.

Each piece of music has its own movement, its own balance, and its own feeling of direction. The careful listener will try to be sensitive to these and, while doing so, will become aware of the various general procedures without becoming deaf to the uniqueness of the individual piece.

So far, we have been describing music by pointing out continuity of movement through similarity and through contrast and the expectations which make that continuity possible. Only occasional, passing references have been made to expressive qualities. It remains to show the way in which musical expression arises out of musical movement and the expectations evoked by that movement. For the elements of melody, harmony, rhythm, texture, tone-color, and dynamics and the organizational principles of return, variation, development, and contrast are all but means to an end.

A distinction must be made between mood and expression in music. Mood—or tone—is that immediately engaging quality which we describe by general terms such as "gay," "sad," "quiet," "agitated," and so on. Since the mood of a musical motive (for instance) is the result of associations many of which are individual and only some of which are communal within any one culture, no two listeners will necessarily describe that mood in exactly the same terms, although the descriptions will be compatible. Where one person may say "serious," another may say "depressing"; but no one, unless he is being facetious, will say "rollicking" of the same motive. Many a person's visual imagination is powerfully aroused by music, and it is when we deal with imagined actions, rather than with moods, that we can easily fall into the error of supposing that music has no common meaning. For instance, the same piece may be described by one person as a battle and by another as a storm. Both these descriptions are of particularized occasions which would give rise to the same generalized mood, which might be described as clangorous and agitated. Put in another way, music has connotation, but it rarely denotes anything.

Given mood, musical expression arises from musical movement and from the expectations colored by mood (or change of mood) which accompany it. When we feel that we understand music, these expectations appear vividly to be in the music itself. In fact, however, they are functions of the listener's experience (the composer is also a listener), and it is for this reason that we need to cultivate close attention to the musical process.

Let us take, as our final example in this chapter, another Prelude by Chopin, the one in B minor, op. 28, No. 6.[11]

The first two bars of the piece establish, let us say, a somber mood, largely by association with the following factors: the slow tempo, the rhythmic and harmonic monotony of the pulsing accompaniment in the treble, the soft dynamics, the minor mode, and the strange melodic line in the bass. This line rises rapidly to a high note,

falls ponderously two steps down the scale,

(the juxtaposition of three heavy notes is important), and sinks slowly to the point from which it started. The rhythm and the line of this melody are decisive in establishing the mood.

As the piece moves on from this beginning, we become aware that the opening melodic motive is moving upward in a sequence. Compare the high points reached through the rising sixteenth-notes in bars 1, 3, and 5:

11. See p. 140.

At its third appearance the motive expands into a longer line than it had at first and the bass is joined in duet by a melodic line in the treble:

Both treble and bass have become melodic, and the reiterated accompaniment figure

etc.

has been suppressed. The phrase ends with an incomplete cadence, emphasized by a rest, in bar 8.

The *general* expectations aroused by these first eight bars must already be familiar. This is an antecedent phrase, which the listener expects to be complemented by a consequent phrase, ending in a complete cadence. (Compare all the pieces discussed so far.) The *particular* expectations are the ones aroused by the peculiarities of this antecedent phrase: the sequential development of the motive (*a, a, a* extended; 2 bars plus 2 bars plus 4 bars), which includes the general rise mentioned above; the disappearance of the accompaniment toward the end; the duet between treble and bass—all these one expects to hear repeated, with a conclusive ending in the consequent.

But the course of the music deviates strongly from the expected one. Although, in bars 9 and 10, we hear the expected beginning, we begin to suspect, in bars 11 and 12, that something is amiss, because the motive has been subtly altered in both rhythm and melody. Our suspicions are confirmed in bars 13 and 14 by the fact that the melody seems unable to progress beyond the point it reached in bar 12. Both attempts, in bars 13 and 14, to get the motive in motion fail. Mere repetition, with failing dynamics, has replaced sequence. There is a fruitful comparison of effect to be made between the mere repetition with failing dynamics here and the sequential repetition with increasing dynamics in "Adeste Fideles." Here there will be no expansion and no upward movement. The monotonous accompaniment persists doggedly; there is no duet. The harmony has moved to a new key, but no cadence has fixed it there. In bar 15, in the original key, the bass continues with the motive which originally occurred in the treble in bar 7.

This motive is repeated at the same pitch (notice that it does not move on) in bar 16 and expands into a cadential figure in bar 17. At the end of that bar we expect to hear the chord which will produce a feeling of finality, the tonic chord; we expect a complete cadence. Instead, at the beginning of bar 18 there is a "deceptive" cadence (the "wrong," the unexpected, chord),[12] and another attempt must be made at a conclusion. This time (in bars 19–22), the attempt is successful, and the phrase is over.

This second phrase has complemented the first, in that it has presented the same motivic material in the same order, and has reached a tonally satisfactory conclusion. But what might be called the more intimate expectations aroused by the antecedent are frustrated in the consequent: the music does not climb out of its starting place; the monotonous accompaniment does not disappear; the treble fails to turn into a lyric line. The progress of the music—its expression— especially in view of its mood, is a despairing one. Nothing could make this more emphatic than the closing bars—the coda—which show the futility of trying to start this melody again—the conclusion has already been reached. Contrast the pleasing, reminiscent effect of the coda in the Prelude in F-Sharp.

Attention to detail and attention to larger form—these will result in understanding of musical movement and expectation, and it is out of such understanding on the part of the listener that musical expression arises.

12. Technically, a submediant instead of a tonic.

3. HARMONY

Certain notions of harmony have already been introduced during the discussion of Chopin's Prelude in F-Sharp Major in the previous chapter. Let us now consider harmony more fully.

Harmony may be defined as (1) the *simultaneous* combination of tones of different pitches and (2) the *successive* sounding of such *combinations*. A *chord* is the name given to two or more different tones sounded simultaneously. A chord is the basic unit of harmony, just as a single note is the basic unit of melody. When we refer to a composer's "harmony," or to the "harmony" of a particular composition, we are referring to the kinds of chords used and to how they succeed one another. When we speak of the theoretical study or science known as "harmony," we are referring to the principles which govern the formation and succession of chords in general. Harmony is sometimes said to be concerned with the *vertical* (or *perpendicular*) dimension of music, melody with the *horizontal*. This analogical distinction is useful, provided we remember that in harmony the progression (necessarily *horizontal*) from one chord to another is as pertinent as is the makeup of any single chord.

If two or more melodies are sounded at the same time, simultaneous combinations of notes of different pitches must occur and succeed each other. Combining melodies was the primary organizational procedure in Western music at least as far back as the twelfth century and for many centuries thereafter, and rules were developed which defined what *intervals* sounded well together or following one another. These rules became essential guides in determining whether particular melodies could or could not be combined or how melodies in combination should move at every point. Nevertheless, in those early centuries, composers thought primarily in terms of the forward movement of the melodies. They asked first, for instance, whether when one melody goes up a step it sounds well for the combining melody to go down a half-step, and they asked only second whether the resulting movement from an interval of, say, a third to an interval of a fifth is good. These composers apparently never thought of intervals (we shall henceforth call them "chords") as moving in accordance with laws capable of elaboration into a generalized theoretical system, independent of particular melodic problems. Late in the sixteenth century, however, at about the same time that the major-minor scales with which we are familiar began to push older scales substantially out of the picture, composers began to realize that such laws existed and that they were in fact being governed by these laws—that they were indeed hearing chords moving in orderly progression just as surely as they were hearing melodies twining and untwining.

The realization of the existence of harmony did not mean that harmony was new. It meant, rather, that the harmonic dimension of music was more vividly present to the composer's mind than it had been before. And, when we speak of harmonic "laws," we are speaking neither of natural necessities (or natural probabilities) nor of regulations imposed from without. We are, rather, referring to normal procedures deduced from the practice of composers. These normal procedures do not remain the same at all times and in all places. They have a history. The reader should understand that only one segment of this history is the source of the information in this chapter, namely, the period between, roughly, 1600 and 1900.

In order to formulate the laws of harmony—or, less ambitiously, to communicate what an analysis of the chordal progression in a particular work might reveal—an additional vocabulary of words and symbols is needed and some sort of structural system, more or less arbitrary, is required as a frame of reference.

A *chord* has already been defined as the name given to two or more different notes sounded simultaneously. For purposes of analysis it is necessary to settle on a certain number of notes as forming the elemental chord. We therefore define this chord as containing three different notes, and we call it a *triad*. It is also helpful to settle on a particular note of the chord as the fundamental one and to describe the other notes of the chord in relation to it. For this purpose, we need a way to describe the various intervals.

An interval is the distance in pitch between two tones. Intervals are called *harmonic* when the two tones sound simultaneously, *melodic* when the two tones sound successively.

Harmonic   Melodic

If you will play middle *C* on the piano with the left hand and then, with the right, play in succession the various other degrees of the C-major scale (*D*, *E*, *F*, etc., up to the next *C*), you will have played successively a unison (the *C* alone), a second (*C–D*), a third (*C–E*), a fourth (*C–F*), a fifth (*C–G*), a sixth (*C–A*), a seventh (*C–B*), and an octave (*C–C*). These are the generic names of the intervals. All intervals, however, occur in various sizes, some of which are regarded as consonant, others as dissonant.

Consonant unisons, fourths, fifths, and octaves occur in only one size; these are called "perfect." Consonant thirds and sixths occur in two sizes; the larger of these are called "major" and the smaller "minor." If you now play all the seconds possible in the C-major scale (*C–D*, *D–E*, *E–F*, etc.), you will discover that they, too, come in two sizes. These are called "major" and "minor." If you do the same with sevenths, you will find them also to be larger and smaller, or major and minor. Seconds and sevenths are classified as dissonances.

Now, a perfect interval or a major interval, when it is made larger by a semitone, becomes "augmented." Likewise, a perfect interval or a minor interval, when it is made smaller by a semitone, becomes "diminished."

In the following example of common intervals, *E* is used as the fundamental note.

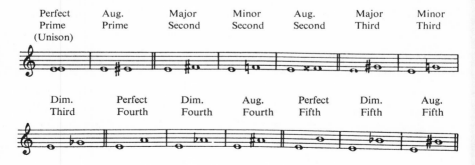

Major	Minor	Aug.	Major	Minor	Dim.	Perfect	Dim.
Sixth	Sixth	Sixth	Seventh	Seventh	Seventh	Octave	Octave

Note that the generic names of intervals (thirds, fifths, etc.) are given without regard to chromatics. For instance, any kind of *G* (sharp, flat, or what not) is a third above any kind of *E*.

The preceding explanation of intervals is intended solely to assist you in reading what follows. Let us revert to the triad. It contains three different notes: one of these is the fundamental note, and the others are described in relation to this fundamental. For reasons both logical and auditory the lowest note is considered the fundamental note or factor, and the chord is thought of as "built up" on this note, which we call the "root" of the chord. We may now limit our description of the elemental chord further and define it as a triad consisting of three factors: a root, the third above the root, and the fifth above the root (*C–E–G*, for example). The triad, so defined and limited, has been the basis of our harmony for several centuries, and, while its dominant position has been considerably undermined in recent times, it is still the starting point for the study of more complex chord formations.

The fourth tone most likely to be added to a triad is the octave above the root (*CEGC*). Since this note can be thought of as merely a recurrence of the root in another register, we feel that essentially all that is present is still the simple triad. Indeed, if we add *E*'s and *G*'s as well as *C*'s from any octave, we consider that what we have is still the triad. Suppose, however, that we add a really different fourth note to the triad: suppose that we build the chord up another third (*G* to *B*), giving us a chord with four different notes (*C–E–G–B*). Such a chord occurs frequently in music. Instead of calling it a "tetrad," however, and asserting that our triad has been superseded, we call it a "chord of the seventh"—the "seventh" refers to the interval between the root and the added top note (*C* to *B*)—and we think of the triad as remaining the primary component of the chord. Keeping the triad, then, as the basis of whatever chords we build up, we may try adding to it any other note or notes whatsoever. But so long as the notes of the triad (*C–E–G*) are not merely being duplicated in other octaves, the result will be a dissonance, that is, a mobile combination of sounds, one which feels as though it should be followed by something else—ultimately, if not immediately, by a triad such as the one with which we started.

In any dissonant combination it is difficult to think merely of the vertical aspect of the harmony, so strong is the implied tendency to move to something else. Although various terminologies have been invented to describe all possible vertical combinations, they have been of little use either in theory or in practice and will be omitted here. When the ear is presented with a dissonance, it is the movement forward from that dissonance to the next chord which is the more vivid experience. That is, we attend to the movements of the various voices which make up the texture; we listen contrapuntally.

But let us return again to the triad and analyze more closely the various forms it may take. A triad, we recall, consists of the root (or fundamental tone), the third above, and the fifth above. These terms identify the factors of a triad in whatever position they actually appear. If the root is the lowest tone, the triad or chord is said to be in *root position;* if the third is the lowest tone, the chord is in the *first inversion.* These forms were the first discovered harmonically, and they make up the main part of the vocabulary of chords. If the fifth is the lowest tone, the chord is in the *second inversion.* In every instance chords are read upward from the bass. Here is a triad built on *C* in root position and in its two inversions, together with chords each of which contains the same three factors as the triad and various octave duplications of them. The effect of the chord in root position is one of stability and completeness in contrast to that of the inversions, especially the second.

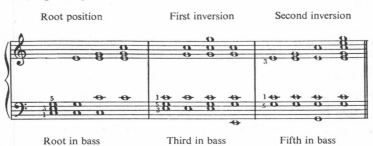

The various intervals formed by the factors of this triad in its three different positions are seen to be the octave, the perfect fifth, the perfect fourth, major and minor thirds, and major and minor sixths. According to traditional theory and practice, these are *consonant* intervals; all other intervals are considered *dissonant.*

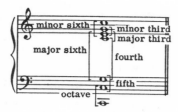

The use of *C* as the root of the chord in our illustrations has been purely arbitrary in order to make things easier. But chords can be, and in analysis have to be, built up with any note of the scale as root. In the *major* and *minor* modes of the key of C, we find these triads:

| I | II | III | IV | V | VI | VII | I | | I | II | III | IV | V | VI | VII | I |

Roman numerals (I–VII) are customarily used to refer both to scale degrees and to chords built upon them. For example, in C, the triad built on *D* is called the "two" chord (II), the triad on *G* the "five" chord (V). The names of the scale degrees are also used to designate chords. Of these, take note of three: the *tonic* (I), the *dominant* (V), and the *subdominant* (IV), since they are the chords most commonly thought of as defining a tonality.

If we study the example above more closely, we may see that the triads based on a given scale differ not only in pitch but also in the size of their intervals. From the relative positions of notes on the staff one might judge all intervals of the same name to be identical, but they are not. In the C-major scale, for example, the interval *C–E* is a *major* third, while *D–F*, which appears to be of the same size as *C–E*, is a *minor* third. The difference is accounted for by the occurrence of a half-step or semitone between *E* and *F*, the third and fourth degrees of the C-major scale. According to the size of the intervals formed between the root and the other two factors, a triad may be *major*, *minor*, *augmented*, or *diminished*. Major triads (I, IV, and V in major) are each composed of a major third and a perfect fifth; minor triads (II, III, and VI in major) are each composed of a minor third and a perfect fifth. These triads are said to be "consonant" chords because they contain only consonant intervals. Diminished triads (such as VII in major) and augmented triads (such as the second III in minor) are said to be "dissonant" because they contain the dissonant intervals of a diminished fifth and an augmented fifth, respectively. The different qualities of these triads are apparent to the ear: major and minor triads sound stable and complete in contrast to the others.

In the example that follows (a familiar hymn simply harmonized in four parts) some of the practical bearings of the foregoing principles are made apparent. The hymn is based on the notes of the C-major scale and is in the key of C major. Each chord is identified functionally by its situation in the key, that is, by the scale degree serving as its root. The subscript numbers (1 and 2) indicate inversions; the number 7 indicates that a fourth note has been added to the triad, making it a chord of the seventh (occurring, as is characteristic of simple harmonizations, only on the dominant—G–B–D–F). In this dominant seventh chord, since there is a fourth factor, a third inversion is possible; when it occurs here it is indicated by the subscript 3.

The harmony throughout consists of but three different chords—the tonic, the dominant, and the subdominant. Each scale degree, and hence each chord, has its part to play in the tonality or key, and the effect of the progression from one chord to the next varies with the chords involved. It will suffice to consider only one such progression—that from V to I, from the dominant to the tonic.

This progression is felt to be particularly strong and satisfying. It occurs in measures 2, 4, 6, and 8, and marks phrase endings. In the last measure it forms what is called a *perfect authentic cadence*, conveying a sense of complete finality. In the other measures the progression is less final in its effect because the third or fifth of the tonic chord is in the soprano (*imperfect* authentic cadence).

Two kinds of perfect cadences (authentic and plagal) are exemplified below together with two other common cadences (*half-cadence* and *deceptive cadence*).

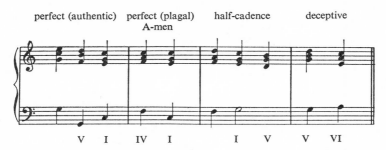

A phrase which ends in a half-cadence requires something else to complete it. In a deceptive cadence the tonic chord, which would normally follow the dominant, is deceptively replaced by another chord.

It would be useful at this point for the reader to review the pieces discussed in the previous chapter, paying particular attention to the effect of the kind of cadence he hears at the end of each phrase. These cadences will have their effect on us when we are listening to music, whether or not we note them and classify them. Paying attention to them, however, assists us in following the form of a work. Moreover, if one becomes thoroughly familiar with the sound of these cadences, he will be the more interested and delighted in hearing progressions in which chromatic alterations occur or in hearing cadences based on modes other than the major and minor.

A cadence is, so to speak, the goal of a phrase. But the sense of movement within the phrase—from dissonance to consonance and from one chord to the next—is more immediate in its effect on the listener. Let us examine an excerpt from a chorale harmonization by J. S. Bach ("Ein' feste Burg"), in order to see again the relationship among dissonance and consonance, harmonic progression within the phrase, and cadence.

Three features of this excerpt will first be briefly discussed: modulation or change of key, the use of "non-harmonic" tones, and the treatment of dissonance. One of the chief sources of harmonic movement is modulation. In measure 2, a modulation occurs from the key of C (the "home" tonic) to the new key of G. This may be said to involve a temporary substitution of the notes of the G scale for those of the C scale; and one evidence of the substitution is the presence of an *F*-sharp in measure two. Modulations are frequently effected by means of "pivot" chords—chords that are common to both the old key and the new. The first chord in measure 2 is such a chord; it is built on *C*, and is both a tonic (I) in the key of C and a subdominant (IV) in the new key of G. It is the door which opens on the new tonal region. The pivot chord is followed by a perfect authentic cadence in the new key. According to the unifying principle of tonality, which requires that a piece begin and end in the same key, a re-modulation takes place and the excerpt (assuming it for the moment to be complete) closes in the original key of C.

Concerning the use of non-harmonic tones, it will be noted that the voice parts, in moving from one chord to the next, introduce notes which are not regarded as a part of the harmonic framework. These notes, originating in the melodic motion of the voice parts, form many dissonant combinations of seconds and sevenths which contribute much to the vitality of the harmonization. Most of these dissonances occur *between* beats and call for no special harmonic treatment. But at the points marked by an asterisk there occur dissonant combinations *on* the beat. The first chord of measure 1 is a triad chord consisting of the notes *F–A–C*, *G* in the alto part being the dissonant note. This note is "prepared" by first appearing as a consonant note in the preceding chord; the dissonance is "resolved" when the *G* drops to *F*, a factor in the chord. Tenor *G* in measure 2 is likewise a dissonant note, and it too is prepared and resolved. Dissonances are not necessarily prepared in all music, however, or even resolved. Music without dissonance would seem lifeless and uninteresting to our ears. It is the dissonant element which helps supply the sense of movement by creating tensions which urge the music on toward a resolution of them. In the foregoing instances the dissonance occurs between two consonances, but often it is not so confined. The treatment of dissonance varies widely from one musical style or period to another.

It would be rewarding to pay close attention to this short Bach excerpt. Listen to it several times until you can actually remember how it sounds. Then notice these things:

1. The way in which the voices move from chord to chord (the "voice-leading," or the contrapuntal aspect of the harmony) tends to make each chord sound like the result of that voice-leading. This is partly because of the dissonance-consonance relationships and partly because of the predominance of stepwise progression (whole-steps and half-steps in the various parts).

2. Because of this kind of voice-leading, the harmonic progressions constantly seem to have direction; they do not wander but progress with force. The harmony moves. The end of its movement in each phrase is a cadence.

3. The two cadences, finally, are related both melodically and harmonically, the second being virtually the same as the first transposed. The first is in the key of the dominant; the second, the tonic. We hear the relationship between these cadences, which are moments of relative repose.

As we listen, then, the smaller movements give rise to larger ones, until a phrase is complete. Finally, the comparison between phrases gives rise to yet a larger sense of movement. Harmony, in both its horizontal and its vertical aspects, is a hierarchy of movement.

4. FORM

In the chapter called "Movement," only two expectations arising from formal procedures were emphasized. First, given a phrase or section which ends either in a new key or with a semicadence in the original key, the listener expects a complementary phrase or section which will end with an authentic cadence in the original key (*A A'*, antecedent and consequent, or *binary form*)[1]; second, given a phrase or section which is tonally complete in itself and is followed by a different phrase or section, the listener expects the first to be repeated (*A B A*, or *ternary form*).[2]

These two procedures are so familiar to us from our musical experience which began in earliest childhood (as *procedures*, not necessarily as *names*), that we may be tempted to think of them as natural.[3] But they are learned. All musical procedures, once following them becomes habitual, seem natural, but all are artificial, although all exemplify the fundamental principles of return, variation or development, and contrast. The importance of knowing the procedures must be obvious from our discussion of the Chopin Prelude in B Minor. But, assuming that one has learned them, how does one know which one is being followed in a particular piece? Occasionally, the title of a piece indicates its procedure, for example, "Fugue," "Rondo," or "Theme with Variations." More often, one's knowledge of style (which will be considered later) leads one

1. First two phrases of the Mozart minuet (expectation not yet fulfilled), first part (*A*) of F-sharp-Major Prelude, B-Minor Prelude, first two phrases of "Londonderry Air," last two phrases of "Londonderry Air," first and second halves of "Adeste Fideles."

2. F-Sharp-Major Prelude, Mozart minuet as a whole (minuet, trio, minuet).

3. With the reader's kind permission, "Twinkle, Twinkle, Little Star," for instance, is ternary; "Rock-a-bye Baby" is binary.

to expect certain procedures in certain contexts, for example, the last movement of a concerto by Mozart will probably be a rondo. Always, however, the behavior of each individual passage in a work, combined with the implications of the way in which the various passages succeed one another, is of primary importance, even when one knows what the general formal procedure is. It is, therefore, to a consideration of this behavior that we now turn.

Our first example will be the second movement of Beethoven's Piano Sonata in C Major, op. 2, No. 3. It is a slow movement in E major.[4]

The piece begins with a theme in two complementary phrases—in binary form (bars 1–4 and 5–8 plus 9 to the beginning of 11), a kind of structure already familiar. The next passage, however, is of a different sort. Not only does it begin with new material and in the minor mode; it also behaves differently. The opening of the piece was a melodic statement—a theme—moving away from and back to a tonal center. It is capable of standing alone because it is internally complete, except for the very last tone of the melody, the omission of which has consequences we shall investigate shortly. But the new passage (bar 11 to the beginning of bar 19) does not stand alone. It moves, tonally, from one place (E minor) to another (G major). Its formal function in the piece as a whole is not to state but to modulate.

In the F-Sharp-Major Prelude of Chopin, there was also a theme followed by a passage incapable of standing alone. But there the passage found its way back to the home tonic. Here the corresponding passage moves to a new tonal region.

In this new region the next passage (bar 19 to the beginning of bar 25) states a new theme, though not one in complementary phrases; here we have a single, complete phrase, followed by its repetition. The key is G major. This theme is the goal of the tonal movement expressed by the modulating passage. (Such a passage is often called a "bridge passage.")

A brief modulatory transition (bar 25) returns the music to E minor and to what begins as a repetition of the modulatory passage encountered previously in bars 11 ff. This time, the course of the movement is different, and the music launches, in bar 37, on a long preparatory passage (bars 37–42). A perhaps more graphic term would be "waiting passage," since the effect of it is one of waiting for the repetition which actually begins in bar 43. In this waiting passage the

4. See p. 141.

bass remains on a single, reiterated note.[5] Amid repetitions of the motive from the G-major theme, this bass note pins down the harmony until it resolves onto a single consonant chord, which lasts for some time before it leads, with a sense of release, into the awaited repetition of the opening theme, in the original key.

But this repetition has a surprising ending in a new key, C major (bars 53–54). From this point until almost the end of the piece (bar 55 to the beginning of bar 77), the music is a condensed and varied repetition of bar 11 to the beginning of bar 53; bar 55 to the beginning of bar 59, a modulatory passage, going this time from C major to E major; bar 59 to the beginning of bar 66, a varied repetition of the theme introduced in bars 19 ff.; bar 67 to the beginning of bar 77, a varied repetition of the opening theme. A brief coda ends the movement.

The functional differences among the various passages in this movement are not only a matter of material, of phrasing, and of tonality; they are emphasized, as well, by differences of texture. There is, for example, a strong difference between the primarily chordal texture of the opening theme, which emphasizes the primacy of the treble melody, and the more equal attraction among the three motivic elements in the succeeding passage:

And when the new theme arrives in bar 19, it is signalized by the imposition of a melodic line upon a continuation of the previous texture, as though an accompaniment had finally discovered what it was that it was supposed to accompany.

What general expectations are aroused in the listener's mind as this piece moves from one section into another? The first section (bar 1 to the beginning of bar 11) is binary and therefore complete in itself except for the omission of the final note of the melody (part *A*). Since something different follows (part *B*), we expect a return to *A*. The first passage in *B*, however, the modulatory passage, moves to a new key and "establishes" it with a cadence; this is a sign that this is not a new theme but that a new theme will follow. The new theme which follows is the kernel of *B*, so to speak. We now expect (*A B A*) a repetition of *A*. But this repetition is postponed by the brief transition (bar 25) followed by the varied re-

5. *B*, the dominant of E major, the key being prepared.

peat of bar 11 to the beginning of bar 19. Postponement of an expected event in a piece of music is very common, as it gives rise to a feeling of tension which can be relaxed in a satisfying way by the ultimate occurrence of that event. In this case the tension is increased by the long preparatory passage—a most specific sign of the return of *A*. Both the length of the passage and the specificity of its meaning are important to the expression here. The expected return of *A* follows. But it leads, without interruption, to the surprising contrast in bars 53–54. The expectation at this point is not specific, but quite vague; something must be done to bring the theme to a satisfactory conclusion. As soon as the next passage is under way, however, we are aware of what the general shape of the sequel will be: another *B*, followed, of course, by another *A*, as though one time around the ternary procedure were insufficient to provide a sense of completion. Why does the process of alternating *A* and *B* sections not go on ad infinitum? This, like most genuinely naïve questions, is far from stupid. It amounts to asking why the piece is complete when it stops. There are two main answers to this question. The first is tonal: when the "kernel" of *B*—the new theme—reappears, it is in the home tonic, E major; the first appearance had been in another key, G major; tonal balance has been reached. In order to make the second answer, we must listen to the consequences of the fact that the opening melody did not reach its expected final note, the tonic.

This seemingly minor omission turns out to be more than a mere means of emphasizing, by shock, the contrast between *A* and *B*.

For memory plays a vital part as we listen to music attentively. When *A* is repeated, we remember that at its first appearance it was not quite finished. We wonder what will happen this time. There is no way of predicting the specific happening: we know only that something will be done about the ending of the theme.

The specific thing that happens at the end of the repetition is surprising, but one is not surprised that something striking occurs at this point, for one is prepared by one's memory of the theme's past. These particular two bars (53 and 54) are most characteristically musical, for, within the context of the piece, they are both strange and familiar: familiar, because they are based upon a familiar idea, the motive with which *A* begins

(cf. );

and strange, because of the abrupt change of key and of dynamics, emphasized by the more restless texture

(cf. ).

Now, as the sequel leads us to expect yet another repetition of *A*, we realize that the theme has accumulated a novel characteristic: a surprise ending which leads away from the home key. As before, we cannot anticipate the particular way in which the repetition will deal with the problem; we know only that the problem will be dealt with. For if it is not, the work will be lacking in that which, for want of a more precise term, we call "logic." And this logic—or call it, if you will, "coherence"—is something without a belief in the presence of which we cannot proceed in our understanding of any work of art.

When, beginning in bar 67, *A* is repeated—in varied form—we are startled by the *ff* interruption in bars 71–72, until we realize that this interruption, with its unexpected dynamics, is what makes it possible, this time, for the theme to conclude. For the theme does not run the danger of again ending as it did in bar 53: it has already included, and, by bar 73, safely passed over, an abruptly loud passage; it has, so to speak, swallowed its danger by anticipating it. Notice in this connection the difference in rhythmic effect between the conclusion of the melody in bars 10 and 52

and the conclusion in bars 76–77.

The smoothing-out of the rhythm adds to our feeling of assurance that the melody will indeed, this time, reach its final note—the tonic. The reaching of the tonic is affirmed in the coda (bars 77–82) by the emphatic answer

which is a simplified version of

in the final bar of the piece to the twice-asked question

in bars 77–79.

If we now ask again why the piece is complete, we can answer not only that tonal balance has been restored, as was pointed out above, but also that the implications of the incomplete ending in bar 11 have been explored in such a way as to allow the theme to arrive at a satisfactory conclusion.

Let us briefly review these implications. In bar 11 the vital tonic note is omitted—implication: watch out for something at least as startling when the theme is repeated; less vivid implication: eventually the "mistake" will be set right. In bar 53 the tonic note is reached, but it is accompanied by the "wrong" chord, and the music has moved abruptly into another key—implication: at least one more repetition of the theme is necessitated in order to set right the "mistake"; more important, perhaps, any further repetition of the theme runs the danger of ending in an equally startling and abrupt manner. But bars 53–54 find their analogue in bars 71–72 of the next repetition, so that the peculiarity (what we have been calling the "mistake") is transferred to the middle of the theme, making it unnecessary for the ending to be peculiar; we might say that the ending has been desensitized. The transference of the *ff* interruption from the ending of the theme to the middle is another example of a musical event which is simultaneously unexpected and "logical."

Several factors have worked together in our brief analysis of this piece. Some are matters of knowledge and perception; others, of memory; together, they give rise to our feelings of expectation.

The matters of knowledge are, in this case, formal procedures—more accurately, the significance of as yet incomplete formal procedures. For instance: given *A B*, what should follow? Later on in the piece, given *A B A B*, what must follow? Or, given a preparatory passage at a certain point in a larger formal procedure, what should follow? Of course, the kind of passage to which one is listening is a matter of perception as well as of knowledge. In the Beethoven piece the passages were differentiated by means of variety of material and texture as well as by behavior.

We have seen the importance of memory in following the fortunes—in being sensitive to the expression—of the opening theme as it reappears in the piece.

Knowledge and memory together allow us to predict the future of any moment in the piece, sometimes quite specifically, more often in only a generalized way (e.g., there will be a repetition of the opening theme which will end with a sense of completion).

In our previous discussion (pp. 32–34) of the Mozart minuet, little more was done with the passage in bars 41–62 than merely to symbolize it, quite dryly, as *b*. If we now revert, briefly, to the minuet (bars 1–93) and listen to it again carefully, we can detect that *b* does not behave in the same manner as do *a* and *a'*. In these latter sections several melodic ideas are stated and restated in such a way that the two sections behave as antecedent and consequent. But the feelings of incompletion and completion thereby aroused are not paralleled in the two passages (bars 41–54 and 54–62) which make up the section we have called *b*.

The first passage (bars 41–54) in *b* does not restate material from *a;* rather, it makes use of it. Compare the beginning motive

with bars 41–50,

in which that motive is extended by repetition and imitation into a ten-bar phrase ending with a cadence in a new key. In bars 50–54, the end of this phrase, somewhat altered, is repeated in yet another key. A passage such as this (bars 41–54) is called a "development." It is tonally restless. It is also less clearly phrased than anything in part *a*. (Compare it, for instance, with the neatness and clarity of the theme in bars 21–28.) The next passage (54–62) is of a sort with which we have already met in the Beethoven. It is a preparatory passage, during which we wait for the repetition which begins in bar 63. The resolution of the harmony is led up to in the last four bars by the direct procedure of having the treble climb to the first note of the melody in bar 63. Throughout this passage, one tone (*D*) is always present in one instrument or the other.

It is the persistence of this tone (which is the dominant of the key) which is chiefly responsible for the preparatory feel of the passage.

We are now in a position to describe more accurately the procedure followed in this minuet (and the same procedure is followed in the trio). It is called "sonata form." What we have referred to as the "antecedent" is called the "exposition," which is characterized by duality of key. The next section is called the "development section," which is usually characterized (as it is here) by restlessness of tonality. The "consequent" is called the "recapitulation," which characteristically remains in the home tonic. Within the exposition, the part in the home tonic is called the "first theme"; in more extended pieces, the "first theme-group." The part in the other key is often called the "second theme"; but, since it almost always (as here) contains more than one theme (bars 21–28, 29–36), it is better called the "second theme-group." A concise and cadentially emphatic passage such as the four bars which here close the exposition is called either a "closing theme" or a "codetta" (little coda).

In the first movement of this same quartet, the reader will find a far more extensive piece which also follows the sonata-form procedure.

We now turn to another piece, the fugue in C minor from the first book of the *Well-Tempered Clavier* by Bach.[6] This piece follows a formal procedure quite different from the procedures followed by the Beethoven and the Mozart pieces. Indeed, its title, "fugue," indicates that procedure.

A fugue is a contrapuntal piece the texture of which consists of a certain number of individual voices. It is based on a short melody called a *subject* which is enunciated at the beginning by one voice alone and then taken up in imitation by the other voices in succession. The imitation is of two sorts: at the same position in the scale (*subject*) and, usually with alterations, at a different position in the scale (*answer*). One or more melodies (*countersubjects*) may or may not accompany the subject or answer whenever it is presented. The section at the beginning during which the subject or answer appears at least once in each voice is called the *exposition*. A section of the fugue which does not include a complete statement of the subject or answer is called an *episode*.

It is characteristic of episodes to move from one tonal point to another, usually by means of modulating sequences. After the exposition it is the normal procedure for *re-entries* of the subject or answer (appearances after the exposition) to alternate with episodes. This general description of fugal procedure has no indication of the number of episodes and re-entries which may occur, because one cannot generalize on their number. Nor can one generalize on the number of voices.

We expect, then, in this piece, to hear each voice enter with the subject (or answer), building up the texture until it reaches the number of voices it is going to have.

The music proceeds as we expect until bar 5, in which an episode begins. This episode develops the "head" (the first few notes) of the subject in a rising sequence. It is, characteristically, a passage of movement, modulating back to the home tonic. Because of the general fugal procedure, we expect this episode to lead into a repetition of the subject. That it is about to do so is signalized at the end of bar 6 by the anticipation of the beginning of the subject.

6. See p. 145.

The subject reappears now in a third voice, and we realize that the episode we have just heard was within the exposition. (An episode within the exposition is sometimes called a "codetta.")

After the entry of the third voice we do not know whether yet another voice will enter or whether (as turns out to be the case) the exposition has concluded. Immediate continuity is characteristically emphasized in fugal procedure instead of (as in the Beethoven movement) sharp differentiation between sections.

The music proceeds directly to another episode which again develops the head of the subject—again in sequence—but, this time, through imitation between the two upper voices over a "running" bass. The general expectation during this episode is that it will be followed by a re-entry of the subject (or answer), but we do not know specifically either when or at what pitch the re-entry will appear. Indeed, it is not until we get to the middle of bar 11 that we are aware that the expected re-entry has already started, since the beginning of the re-entry is a further member of the sequence developed in the episode. This is another example of the expressive possibilities—the variety of significance—inherent in one's expectations as one listens to music: this re-entry is reached with one meaning (further development—further sequential modulation) and continued with another (restatement in a new key, the goal of the previous episode's movement).

The next episode is the first (and, it turns out, the only) passage in the fugue from which the incisive rhythm of the head of the subject is absent. It provides the strongest textural and rhythmic contrast in the piece. Tonally, it modulates from E-flat back to C minor, where we expect a re-entry in the home tonic. This re-entry, however, is of the answer rather than of the subject, and the key therefore becomes G minor (cf. bars 3–4), keeping the tonality unexpectedly afield.

The next episode is a three-voiced version of the codetta. Since we remember the course of the codetta, we expect this episode to end similarly. In the middle of bar 18, however, there is a sudden pause in the rhythmic flow, followed by an abrupt lowering of the register and a shift of key from G minor to C minor. As the reader can hear, the re-entry of the subject, now again in the home tonic, in bar 20 is a natural continuation of the top line of the texture in the episode—a continuation denied at the corresponding point in bar 18:

The piece now continues into an episode which corresponds to the one which followed the exposition. That one, we remember, moved away from the home tonic to another key. We expect a similar movement here. But at the decisive point (at the beginning of bar 24) a strong dissonance and its sequel

instead of the expected

bring about a return to C minor and, after a brief passage (reminiscent of the codetta) which firmly establishes that key, the subject again. This time, the end of the subject is followed by a sudden silence—a sign of impending conclusion. After a forceful and positive authentic cadence the tonic is sustained in the bass (a "tonic pedal"),[7] and, over it, the subject appears for the last time. There is, in this coda, a change of texture brought about not only by the tonic pedal but also by the fact that the subject, instead of being contrapuntally accompanied, is

7. The preparatory passages in the Mozart and Beethoven pieces we discussed have "dominant pedals."

harmonized. The concluding chord, in accordance with the normal procedure of Bach's time, is major (the "Tierce de Picardie"). The conclusive nature of the coda is, then, the result of a combination of factors: the preceding pause, the authentic cadence, the extra repetition of the subject, the more homophonic texture, and the final major triad.

The particular form of this particular piece should be sharply distinguished from the general procedure, as was done in our discussion of the Beethoven slow movement. This particular form is the result chiefly of two factors: tonality and the sequence of events. Let us consider them together.

In the exposition we hear first the subject, then the answer—C minor and G minor. The answer is followed by an episode (the codetta) which returns us to the subject—C minor. The subject is succeeded by an episode which modulates to E-flat, in which key there is a re-entry. So far, the musical flow has been easy, although rhythmically vigorous, and the emphasis has been on unhampered continuity. But now a relatively strong contrast is introduced (bars 13–14) which not only breaks the ease of continuity but also threatens to bring the music abruptly back to C minor before it has been fairly launched on its tonal journey. The threat is avoided by the re-entry of the answer, which keeps the tonality away from home—G minor. But now the previous course of the music reasserts itself. What happened previously after the answer in G minor? Then what happened? And so on. A comparison of that portion of the fugue from bar 3 to the episode beginning in bar 13 with the portion going from bar 15 through bar 28 will show the importance here of parallel development. For, once we recognize the familiar, we expect its familiar sequel. As the codetta is remembered to have moved from G minor back to C minor, we expect the episode beginning in bar 17 to do likewise. But it so behaves that, unless violence is done to it, it will remain in G minor. That violence is indeed done—in the middle of bar 18. The expected modulation from G to C has occurred, but it has been effected dramatically. However, the return to the home tonic comes too soon for the completion of the sequence of events. The music continues (bar 22) as expected, with an episode corresponding to the one in bars 9–10. But it cannot be allowed to move freely as it did before; the home tonic has asserted its rights. Therefore, the strong dissonance in bar 24 and the powerful return to C minor, reinforced by the re-entry in bars 26–28. It is significant that, at the corresponding place in the first portion, the episode slipped insensibly into the re-entry (bar 11); here, the point at which the re-entry begins (middle of bar 26) is emphasized by the harmonic preparation which precedes it.

In retrospect, we can see that the unique episode (bars 13–14) is the pivotal point in the form. Notice the correspondence of the two portions we have been comparing (S = subject; A = answer; ep. = episode):

S (C mi.)	A (G mi.)	codetta	S (C mi.)	ep. I	S (E-flat ma.)
			ep. II		
	A (G mi.)	ep. III	S (C mi.)	ep. IV	S (C mi.)	coda

Notice also that the first portion develops toward E-flat but that the second portion restores tonal balance by returning to C.

In a diagram such as this the form looks rather tame. No hint is given of the way in which the easy flow of the first portion is replaced by the forcible—even wilful—movement of the second. Nor is there any indication of the variation in effect achieved by the placement of the subject and answer, in their recurrences, in various parts of the texture: top, middle, and bottom. This variety of placement is made possible by the fact that the subject and the two countersubjects which accompany it can be put in any vertical order that the composer desires; they are in so-called "invertible counterpoint."

In the Beethoven and Bach pieces we have now studied two examples of the interplay among various factors: general procedure, specific behavior of individual passages, textural differentiation, and the effect of memory. Although we applied the same method to our study of each piece, a gross comparison might be illuminating.

The Beethoven tends to develop by contrast, with the various sections well set off one from another by differences of thematic material, texture, and behavior. The Bach tends to develop by similarity: the various sections, although well set off from one another by behavior, are only subtly differentiated in thematic material and texture (with the exception of the pivotal episode in the middle). In keeping with this difference—and not merely because of the slower tempo—the Beethoven takes longer to develop than the Bach. Put in another way, Bach's music happens faster. This is so because contrast in general needs more room than does similarity, in order that the developing problems may reach a satisfying solution.

The similarity latent in this comparison is of great importance: both pieces contain passages differentiated from one another by behavior. There is a valid analogy between subject, answer, and re-entry versus episode, on the one hand, and theme versus modulatory passage and preparatory passage, on the other. The analogy lies in the difference between statement—goal of movement or its point of departure—and movement toward such a goal or away from such a point of departure.

The importance of this similarity lies in the fact that, given a knowledge of the general formal procedure, the behavior of the individual passage, along with one's memory of what has gone before it, is the key to one's understanding of the individual progress of any piece of music. And it is one's sensitivity to that progress that is the chief source of musical expression.

There is one important kind of passage, the introduction, which is not illustrated by any of the pieces we have so far considered. A superb example of a slow introduction to an allegro in sonata form may be found in the first movement of Beethoven's Piano Sonata in C Minor, op. 111. Here tonal suspense is finally resolved in a passage of preparation which leads into the exposition. In Rimsky-Korsakov's *Capriccio espagnol*, which will be considered later, the "Gipsy Dance" has an introduction which combines rhapsodic passages with anticipations of the dance itself. But the only generalization one can make about the meaning of introductions is that they combine a sense that a clear procedure is about to occur with a feeling of suspense with respect either to the nature of the material in the ensuing movement (as in the Beethoven) or to the moment when that movement will begin (as in the Rimsky-Korsakov)—or to both.

We have been discussing pieces in which general procedures are followed. But what if a general procedure, though set up, is not followed? Or, what if more than one procedure is set up? The answers to these questions have one thing in common, namely, that a particular expressive effect is being sought and that this effect depends upon one's knowledge of general procedures. Let us briefly discuss two final examples, one to illustrate each question.

The first example is the bass air, "Why do the nations so furiously rage together?" No. 40 in Handel's *Messiah*. We hear first a self-contained section in C major, to the text: "Why do the nations so furiously rage together? And why do the people imagine a vain thing?" This is followed by another section which begins in A minor and moves to E minor, coming to a solid conclusion in that key. The text of this section is: "The kings of the earth rise up, and the rulers take counsel together against the Lord, and against His Anointed." The procedure is that of the *aria da capo—A B A*—and we have heard parts *A* and *B*. We now expect to hear a repetition of part *A*. Instead, the chorus (No. 41) bursts in with a vigorous and enthusiastic contrapuntal treatment, to new music, of the words: "Let us break their bonds asunder, and cast away their yokes from us." Why? The answer obviously lies in the meaning of the text, which the composer has here treated in dramatic fashion. In the first part of the aria a question has been asked about a political situation eternally with us. In the second part the cause of that situation has been pointed to in the impious actions of rulers. The remedy—to free ourselves from that kind of ruler—suggests itself immediately to the chorus (which stands here for mankind), and they shout it out; they cannot wait for the bass to repeat his description; they cut him off.

Now, there is no doubt that these two numbers are tremendously dramatic to those who do not realize that they are hearing a *da capo* aria made incomplete by the precipitate intrusion of a chorus. But the effect is redoubled when one expects one thing and hears another. There is not only surprise; there also is a sense of satisfaction with the rightness of that surprise. A quieter aspect of that satisfaction is derived from the tonality of the chorus, which is C major, the key the *da capo* would have had.

Our other example is the finale of the Mozart Quartet in G Major, the minuet from which we have already discussed. As this movement begins, we are plainly listening to a fugue. But no sooner is the exposition over than the most un-fugue-y of "episodes" takes place. It is not merely not very contrapuntal in texture; it is positively anticontrapuntal. What sort of procedure can this be? Not only is the texture uncompromisingly homophonic; the phrasing is distinct, and the whole passage is repeated. Its ending then becomes the leading motive of the highly contrapuntal modulatory passage which follows. No sooner has this passage reached the dominant of the new key (D major) than it is succeeded by a long dominant preparation—again homophonic. Next, in the new key, comes another fugal exposition, on a new subject. Then yet another, in which the two subjects are combined—a double-fugal exposition. Still in the new key, a new tune, clearly phrased, with chordal accompaniment, follows, to be succeeded by one of those passages of conclusion such as we met with earlier in bars 37–40 of the minuet in this same quartet. Thereupon, everything we have so far heard is repeated. It is now clear that a fugal procedure is being married to a sonata-form procedure at the point of a shotgun. In the abstract, there is nothing inherently funny about this combination, but the composer has chosen to treat the dual personality of his piece as a paradox and as an expression of wit and high good humor. For, instead of blending the two, he has brought out the differences between them.[8] The rest of the movement carries out the implications fully. The highest contrast is saved for the coda: a stretto[9] on the opening fugue subject, followed shortly by a harmonization of it in block chords by way of conclusion.

The procedures of which we have been speaking are learned by induction and by comparison, and every fresh case adds to one's understanding. There are, however, certain remarks which can truthfully be made about each of them. In order for the reader to get a start in the right direction when he first meets a new piece, therefore, those procedures which he is most likely to find in the music he hears are described under "Common Procedures and Types."[10]

We are now in a position to expand our notion of rhythm in the light of our discussions in this section.

Rhythm in its broadest sense embraces not only such factors as meter, tempo, and groupings of notes but also the patterned recurrence of larger units. Just as beats are grouped into measures, so measures are grouped into phrases, which are in turn grouped into larger units of rhythm. Since music unfolds in time, it is experienced as a flux of related moments, and its form comes only as a gradual revelation to the listener. At any given instant in the course of a musical work the attentive listener's consciousness holds, together with the immediate perception, a unified impression of that portion of the music already heard and an expectancy regarding what is to come. In this interplay of present, past, and future lies the listener's sense of the larger rhythm.

8. For a quite different sort of piece using the same two procedures listen to the finale of Haydn's Quartet in F Minor, op. 20, No. 5.

9. For a definition of *stretto*, see p. 107.

10. See pp. 101 ff.

5. COLOR

The various musical instruments necessarily use a common pitch vocabulary. Their function so far as pitch is concerned is the production of tones that conform to the chromatic scale. One might say that this scale is "built into" keyboard and wind instruments, while most stringed instruments and the human voice are more or less confined to it because of the traditional technique of playing and singing. But so far as quality or timbre is concerned, the emphasis falls not on what the various instruments and voices have in common but on the unique contribution of each. For example, both the flute and the clarinet are designed to produce tones of very different quality. A note of given pitch, loudness, and duration played on the flute differs markedly from the same note played on the clarinet. The varieties of tone used in our music are many. Not only do we possess a large number of different musical instruments, each with its individual quality of tone, but instruments of the same type vary, and performers on them differ. Differences among singing voices are as apparent to the ear of the connoisseur as are differences of physiognomy to the eye.

Most musical instruments are equipped with a means for altering the frequency of their vibrating parts so that they can produce tones of different pitches. Lacking such a means, they would in fact be practically useless for most musical purposes. Some instruments have individual strings, pipes, or bars for each tone, as is true of the piano, the organ, and the xylophone, respectively. Instruments of the violin family and other stringed instruments produce a number of tones on each of their several strings through alterations of the vibrating lengths of those strings. And such instruments as the flute, trumpet, and clarinet produce a number of tones on a single tube by various mechanical devices. Some of the more important means for the production and control of tones of different pitches may now be briefly outlined.

The frequency of vibration of a stretched string depends upon four factors— the length and diameter of the string, its tension or degree of tautness, and the material of which it is made. In the piano these factors are fixed for each string, though they necessarily vary from one string to another. In a violin that is tuned and ready for playing, all factors are fixed except the one which can be most easily and rapidly controlled, namely, the length of the string, which the player can vary by means of his fingers. If the player shortens the *A*-string, for example, by one-ninth its length, the pitch will rise to *B;* if he shortens it by one-fifth its length, the pitch will rise to *C*-sharp; and so on through successive shortenings of one-fourth for *D*, one-third for *E*, two-fifths for *F*-sharp, seven-fifteenths for *G*-sharp, and finally one-half for *A*, the octave above the starting note. Each shortening of the string causes an increase in frequency and hence a rise in pitch. Halving the string doubles the frequency, so that if our starting note *A* has a frequency of 440 vibrations per second, the *A* an octave higher will have a frequency of 880 vibrations per second. So far as the control of pitch alone is concerned, one might say that the technique of violin playing is the art of accurately shortening strings to the desired vibrating lengths.

In wind instruments the method used to produce tones of different pitches does not differ essentially from that used in instruments of the violin family. Wind instruments have this feature in common: instead of strings, the sounding medium is an inclosed column of air which is made to pulsate by some vibrating agent—the compressed lips of the player, a reed, or a sharp edge against which a stream of air is blown. The oboe, English horn, and bassoon are double-reed instruments; clarinets are single-reed. Piccolo and flute are cross-blown; all other wood winds and brasses are end-blown. Change of pitch is effected by altering the working length of the tube or pipe which incloses the column of air. The slide trombone affords us the clearest example of this principle in operation. As its name suggests, this instrument is equipped with a metal sleeve which slides over its main tube so that the player can alter the length of the inclosed air column at will. Similarly, a trumpet has three permanently attached crooks or pieces of tubing which can be added to the effective length of the instrument by means of piston valves. The player of a trumpet, trombone, or other "brass" instrument initiates the tone by blowing into a cup-shaped mouthpiece a stream of air which is broken up into periodic puffs by his vibrating lips. In the clarinet, periodic puffs of air enter the instrument through the action of a vibrating reed which alternately opens and closes a slit through which the player blows. Holes bored in the side of the clarinet serve the same purpose as the slide of the trombone and the crooks of the trumpet; they are means by which the player can alter the working length of the instrument and so control frequency of vibration. An elaborate apparatus of keys and connecting rods is used in the clarinet and other "wood-wind" instruments to facilitate the opening and closing of these lateral openings, which may in some cases be too far apart for the human hand, or too large to be stopped by the finger tips. Since the principle of shortening a tube is precisely the same as that of shortening a string, it is to be expected that the nearer the holes are to the mouthpiece of the instrument, the higher will be the pitch when they are opened. The human voice may be regarded as a sort of reed-pipe instrument in which the vocal cords act as a double reed, and the nose, mouth, and throat as a resonating pipe. The pitch of the voice depends mostly upon the length and tension of the vocal cords. As we have seen, frequency varies inversely with length, and so, if a man's vocal cords are half an inch long, a woman's may be perhaps a third shorter, and a child's much shorter still. The flute presents no new features beyond those already discussed except that its air column is made to pulsate by means of a flat stream of air directed against the sharp edge of a mouth-hole or flue cut in the side of the instrument near the end. In this case the vibrating agent is the air itself and not a string, reed, or membrane.

It is true of wind instruments generally that they can produce many tones of different pitches (specifically, the chromatic scale) even though they have comparatively few lateral openings, keys, or pistons. A piano has eighty-eight keys for the sounding of the same number of notes. A violin has four differently pitched strings, each of which may be shortened to any desired vibrating length. But a trumpet has only three pistons by which to produce about thirty different tones within its normal range. And, similarly, a trombonist employs only seven different slide positions for the production of many times that number of notes. The explanation for this lies in the fact that a pipe or tube can, without its working length being changed, be made to sound a number of different tones through a process called "overblowing." That is, by altering the tension of his lips and the pressure of his breath, the player can induce the inclosed column of air to pulsate in halves, thirds, etc., and so to produce, within limits, the various tones of the harmonic or overtone series.[1] Since these "overblown" notes do not form a scale (the intervals between them being too large), an instrument such as the bugle, which lacks a device for varying the length of its air column, cannot play even so simple a tune as "America."

In some instruments of the percussion family elastic bars or plates are used as sound-producing agents. The pitch of these, if they have determinate pitch, depends partly upon their size and shape and partly upon the material of which they are made. Solid bodies of this sort cannot be readily altered in shape or length, and hence they must be used in series if the instrument is to be capable of sounding tones of different pitches. The tension of a membrane, however, can be altered. For example, the kettledrum consists of a membrane stretched over the open end of a metal bowl. Change of pitch is effected by increasing or lessening the tension of the membrane.

Other means for the production and control of tones of different pitches are now being developed in the form of instruments which make use of electrical impulses instead of vibrating strings, reeds, pieces of metal or wood, membranes, or columns of air. While most electronic instruments are not yet in widespread use, they will doubtless continue to grow in importance as they are perfected and as musicians realize their potentialities. In general, these instruments make use of the heterodyne principle of combining two electric currents, either of whose frequencies is far beyond the limits of audibility but whose difference frequency can be amplified into sound. (Whenever two tones sound simultaneously, they give rise to a third tone whose frequency is equal to the difference between their frequencies.) By varying the frequency of one or both of the currents, the difference frequency will become larger or smaller, producing correspondingly higher or lower pitches.

We have been assuming that a musical sound is a simple, "pure" tone of a single definite pitch. Actually a musical sound consists of a combination of tones of different pitches, called *harmonics* or *partials*, which all sound together. The harmonic of lowest pitch is the *fundamental;* the harmonics above it are *overtones.* The fundamental is ordinarily so strong as to dominate the overtones and to establish its pitch as the pitch of the composite sound. When the note *A* is

1. See below, p. 75.

said to have a frequency of 440 vibrations per second, the frequency referred to is that of the fundamental, while the frequencies of the overtones are ignored. It is quite possible through concentrated listening to detect some of the constituent tones of a musical sound which to the uninitiated ear is simple and pure. If a low C is sounded vigorously on the piano, the fundamental will at first seem to be the only audible harmonic; but if one concentrates on hearing sounds higher than C, some of the more prominent overtones—the second G above, for example—will emerge so conspicuously as to render incredible the fact that they were previously unnoticed. The vibrations which produce noise are irregular and relatively complex; no continuous fundamental is discernible, and the partials are inharmonious and unstable in their relationships. The very different character of the vibrations which produce a musical sound may be judged from what follows.

Experiments show that a sounding body such as a stretched string or a column of air vibrates not only as a whole but also in many fractional parts, each partial vibration producing an overtone. Let us suppose that the C-string of a violoncello is vibrating at a frequency of 64 vibrations per second, which is the frequency of the fundamental or first harmonic. At the same time, the string vibrates in halves at twice the frequency of the fundamental (128), producing the second harmonic (first overtone); it also vibrates in three equal parts at triple the frequency of the fundamental (192), producing the third harmonic (second overtone); and so on indefinitely. The frequencies of the different harmonics stand in the simple ratios $1:2:3:4:5:6$, etc., corresponding to the string's vibrating as a whole, in halves, thirds, fourths, fifths, sixths, etc. For example, the tenth harmonic results from a division of the string into ten separately vibrating parts and has a frequency ten times that of the fundamental (640).

The first sixteen harmonics of the harmonic series of cello C are given below in musical notation—first, in chord form to indicate that they occur simultaneously, and then in succession. The numbers above the notes indicate the frequencies of the various harmonics; the consecutive numbers below the notes indicate the position of each harmonic in the series, the fundamental being 1, the first overtone 2, the second overtone 3, and so on. It should be noticed that the number of any harmonic is also the number of parts into which the whole string divides itself in order to produce that harmonic. The notes inclosed in brackets are only approximations of pitches used in our scale.

The overtones of any musical sound always preserve these simple relationships to one another and to the fundamental, regardless of what the fundamental is. For example, if the C-string of the cello were shortened by a certain portion of its length, the pitch would rise to C-sharp, and the entire harmonic structure would be shifted up correspondingly without any change in frequency ratios or intervallic relationships. As before, the frequency ratio of the first two harmonics would be 2:1, and the interval formed by these harmonics would necessarily be the octave.

Let us now suppose that a bassoon sounds the same low C as the cello. How is the difference in tone quality to be accounted for? The bassoon C and the cello C necessarily have two things in common: their fundamental frequencies are identical, and their harmonics conform to the same series. The difference in tone quality arises partly from the fact that each instrument makes its own selection of overtones from the series and gives them varying intensities. For example, the highest harmonics present in the string C are virtually absent from the bassoon C, while the third harmonic of the latter is relatively prominent. The "pure" tone of the flute lacks or is weak in all harmonics except the fundamental and first overtone; the strong predominance of odd-numbered harmonics has to do with the mellow timbre of the clarinet; the pungent, reedy quality of the oboe tone springs largely from the intensity pattern of its many overtones; the higher harmonics (above the sixth or seventh) of the trumpet tone are stronger than the lower and help create its sharp and penetrating quality. Tone quality may vary quite widely from one register of an instrument to another. We speak of the "chalumeau," middle, and high registers of the clarinet, and yet, different as these are, a characteristic "clarinet" quality is present in all three. According to recent theory, the underlying sameness of quality in different registers of an instrument is due to the *formant* of the instrument—the absolute range to which its characteristic overtones are confined regardless of the pitch of the fundamental.

Necessary to every tone-producing instrument is a resonator—a means of reinforcing the tones initiated on the instrument. A piano without a soundboard to reinforce the vibrations of its strings would produce tones of little or no musical value. The strings of a violin, if removed from the instrument and stretched at their usual tension, would in vibrating emit only the feeblest of sounds. If a wind-instrument player detaches the mouthpiece from his instrument and attempts to sound it in the ordinary manner, he can at best produce only a weak buzzing noise. This is so because the pipe or tube of the instrument not only "works back" to control the vibrations of the lips or reed but also acts as a *resonator*. The celesta and in some cases the xylophone have wooden resonators attached to each of their bars to reinforce and sustain their tones.

Each resonator has free vibrations of its own. For instance, when a clarinet is played, not only the column of air inside the instrument vibrates, but also the tube itself. And this tube's own vibrations are a complex of frequencies which do not have the simple relationships to one another of tones in the harmonic series but which are grouped together in a frequency range considerably higher than the range of the tones the instrument is designed to produce. A group of frequencies belonging to an instrument's resonator is called the *formant* of that instrument.

Since an instrument's formant is higher in frequency range than the tones played on the instrument, some of the harmonics of those tones will fall into the range of the formant. Therefore, every instrument emphasizes constantly those harmonics which fall into that range. It is this tendency of resonators to emphasize certain groups of frequencies that appears to be the chief source of individual tone-colors. An interesting example of the properties of a formant is the case of the triangle. This is an instrument of indefinite pitch—that is, it has no single fundamental pitch which is *the* pitch of the instrument—but it manages to sound in tune in any harmonic context. It can do this because its formant allows it to resonate with whatever very high harmonics are being produced by the other instruments around it.

Ordinarily we do not hear overtones separately; we hear them merely as constituents of what the ear accepts as a single sound. The disappearance of some, the addition of others, an alteration in their relative intensities—these are perceived as changes in quality of tone. But in wind instruments overtones can be produced separately by the process previously referred to as "overblowing." The French horn, for example, can by a competent player be made to sound in succession all the lower overtones in the harmonic series without the length of its tube being altered. We must first suppose that the French horn is sounding *C*, the *second* harmonic, since owing to its narrow bore it cannot produce the fundamental. This *C*, like all horn notes, is very rich in overtones, and these are all sounding together, giving the note its peculiar horn quality. If the player now increases the tension of his lips, he can make the air column pulsate in thirds of its length, producing *G* (the third harmonic); in fourths, producing *C* (the fourth harmonic); and so on up to the sixteenth harmonic. Presumably, if he were more than human, he could force the instrument up as high as the thirtieth harmonic. With a single length of tubing, then, the horn player has a variety of pitches at his command. Since the French horn, unlike the bugle, has valves by which extra lengths can be added to its tube, the player is able to fill in the gaps between the harmonics of the original series. He can, in other words, play a complete chromatic scale. The violinist, by lightly touching a string instead of stopping it in the usual manner, can produce harmonics on the violin, sometimes called "flageolet tones" because of their high flutelike timbre. The touch of a finger at a third of the length of the string, for example, while preventing the string from vibrating as a whole (and hence no fundamental is heard) causes the string to vibrate in three segments, producing the third harmonic. It is of course necessary that the string be *lightly* touched so that it is free to vibrate on *both* sides of the dividing point. Producing harmonics on a violin is in principle the same as overblowing a wind instrument.

The history of the orchestra, its standardization through a process of evolution and selection, can be only briefly suggested here.

Until about 1600, instrumental music was largely vocal in style; consequently, a premium was put upon such instruments as could easily carry a vocal line. The strings were the backbone of the orchestra for this reason. They have never lost their position.

The wood winds came in one by one as they improved mechanically and were discovered to be capable of carrying a melodic part. Their importance as melodic instruments remains second only to the strings. At first they doubled with strings; later they frequently were assigned alternate melodic sections of a work in order to contrast with the strings; in the nineteenth century their individual color was exploited and an individual idiom was discovered for each instrument.

The brass instruments came into the orchestra later than the wood winds. The melodic value of the horn was early discovered, but trumpets and trombones served chiefly to reinforce climaxes of massed sound. Except for the trombone, they did not become fully satisfactory mechanically until the nineteenth century; nor until then was the full chromatic scale—not simply the harmonics of their fundamental tone—available to all of them. Both wood winds and brasses had been useful for the filling-out of the chords of the harmony; except for the high trumpet and the horn, however, the coloristic possibilities of brasses as well as wood winds was a nineteenth-century discovery.

Though the timpani became a staple of early orchestras because of the rhythmic basis they offered, the full variety of percussion instruments came into the orchestra only in the nineteenth century, with the interest in color and in national rhythms.

With the late symphonies of Haydn the framework of the orchestra may be said to be standardized (ca. 1790). The nineteenth century simply reinforced and filled in the standard structure. It also provided the large concert hall and the conductor who stands up in front of the orchestra with a stick, in contrast to the earlier practice of having a player conduct the group, first, from his place at the harpsichord or piano, next, from the first-violin desk. Our twentieth-century virtuoso conductors and our full orchestras are essentially a nineteenth-century phenomenon. Composers of the present century, however, are tending to break the standard pattern, writing for unusual combinations of instruments, usually smaller combinations, undermining the autonomy of the separate choirs, and cutting the orchestra away to some extent from its solid basis, the string choir.

The size of the modern symphony orchestra is not standardized. A so-called "major" orchestra, however, will have approximately 108 players (see p. 79). It is not the convention of orchestras to list their players in the order given. Personnel lists almost always begin with the first violins, then follow through with the other strings. First on the whole list is the "concertmaster," that is, the outside player at the first desk of first violins. The order of "choirs" and instruments in our listing follows that in which they are conventionally arranged on an orchestral score, with the piccolo and flutes at the top, string basses at the bottom, and the others in between in the order given.

It is unnecessary to specify here the range of pitch of each of the instruments. In general, it may be said that *within each choir* the listing of the instruments here (and on a score) is roughly in order of range, from highest pitches down to lowest, although in the brass choir the trumpet is higher in pitch than the horn. The list fails to indicate, however, that for certain instruments there are two or more varieties available, with different ranges of pitch. There are, for instance, a tenor trombone and a bass trombone, a tenor tuba and a bass tuba.

Wood winds (16)
  1 piccolo
  3 flutes
  3 oboes
  1 English horn[2]
  3 clarinets
  1 bass clarinet
  3 bassoons
  1 contra-bassoon
Brasses (18)
  8 horns[2] (French horn)
  5 trumpets
  4 trombones
  1 tuba

Percussion (5)
  2 timpani
  3 percussion
Miscellaneous (3)
  2 harps
  1 piano
Strings (66)
  18 first violins
  16 second violins
  12 violas
  10 violoncellos
  10 basses (double-bass)

This list of performers in a modern symphony orchestra is misleading in that an important difference, in general, between strings and all the other choirs is not noted. All 18 first violins play the same part, the same notes—except in those instances in which the composer explicitly calls for them to be divided ("divisi") or for only certain desks to play. Similarly with the 16 second violins, etc. But when a composer calls for 3 flutes, he customarily writes a separate part, different notes, for each of these flutes. When he calls for 2 bassoons, there is a separate part for each; 3 trombones, unlike 10 cellos, means not one part but a part for first trombone, one for second trombone, and one for third trombone. Similarly for 2 harps, etc. Except for the bowed strings, that is, every instrument

2. The reader should be cautioned against confusing *horn*, which always means the French horn, a brass instrument, with the English horn, a wood-wind instrument with an oboe quality more pronounced than that of the oboe itself. The reader should be warned also against making a present-day distinction between wood winds and brasses on the grounds of the material of which the instruments are made. Originally such a distinction existed and gave rise to the generic names of the choirs, but flutes, regularly, and other "wood-wind" instruments, occasionally, are today constructed of metal.

plays a separate "line" (not necessarily a separate staff on the full score, however; the winds are usually grouped two to a staff).

After establishing firmly the contrast between the division of parts among strings and among the instruments of the other choirs of the orchestra, we must retreat and dispel the notion that wind instruments never "double" on a part or that composers have never expected them to do so. Composers often call for doubling in places where the character of the part is not soloistic and where doubling is desirable for volume, timbre, or balance. (The indications "a 2," "a 3," etc., call for doubling.)

To understand the growth of the orchestra, it is helpful to compare the instrumentation of four works separated in time. "Strings" in these instrumentations means first violins, second violins, violas, cellos, and basses. The division of the strings is uniform, although the number of players on each part has increased along with the multiplication of parts in the other choirs.

Haydn, *Symphony No. 104 in D Major* ("London") (1795): 2 flutes, 2 oboes, 2 clarinets, 2 bassoons, 2 horns, 2 trumpets, timpani, and strings.

Weber, Overture to *Der Freischütz* (1820): 2 flutes, 2 oboes, 2 clarinets, 2 bassoons, 4 horns, 2 trumpets, 3 trombones, timpani, and strings.

Wagner, *Tristan und Isolde* (1865): 3 flutes, 1 piccolo, 2 oboes, 1 English horn, 2 clarinets, 1 bass clarinet, 3 bassoons, 4 horns, 3 trumpets, 3 trombones, 1 tuba, timpani, cymbals, triangle, harp, and strings, plus extra trumpets, trombones, and horns on the stage.

Mahler, *Symphony No. 9* (1909): 4 flutes, 1 piccolo, 3 oboes, 1 English horn, 3 clarinets, 1 E♭ clarinet, 1 bass clarinet, 3 bassoons, 1 contra-bassoon, 4 horns, 3 trumpets, 3 trombones, 1 tuba, timpani, bass drum, cymbals, triangle, tam-tam, chimes, glockenspiel, snare drum, 2 harps, and strings.

The reader will notice that two of these scores (the Wagner and the Mahler) call for more players than there are in the list given previously. Indeed, there are a good many works which require the services of extra musicians.

The instruments of the orchestra evolved from earlier instruments; they were also selected from a great number of other instruments available at the time that the orchestra was developing. The vast number of ancient, medieval, Renaissance, and Baroque instruments, now obsolete, and of present-day national or folk instruments, or other instruments not belonging to the symphony orchestra, cannot be discussed here. All of them employ in one form or another one of the methods of tone production discussed earlier. Certain of the old, supposedly obsolete instruments are revived from time to time, however, or we encounter music originally written for them, so that a brief description of a few of them here may be useful.

In the Renaissance and Baroque[3] periods, "viola" was the generic Italian name for all bowed-string instruments. The most important early classification was the separation of all viols into either *viole da braccia*, meaning "arm-viols," played somewhat in the position the violin is played in today, and *viole da gamba*, meaning "leg-viols," played somewhat as the cello is played today. These two instruments differed in shape, the back of the gamba being flat, its shoulders sloping, its openings crescents rather than f-shaped. Each fathered a family of instruments running through all sizes and ranges, and it is from the braccia family that our violin, viola, and cello are derived. The gambas lacked volume; their tone was cooler and slightly nasal. The influence of the gamba survives today only in the double-bass, which combines features of both families. As late as the middle of the eighteenth century, however, one member of the gamba family remained an active competitor of the cello and is occasionally revived today: the six-stringed *viola da gamba*, tuned *D, G, c, e, a, d'* (*d'* is one note above middle *c*). This gamba is played with the hand underneath the bow—rather than over the bow as are violin, viola, and cello. The finger boards of gambas were originally fretted, that is, the positions for placing the fingers were marked with narrow strips of wood or metal.

The *viola d'amore* was an eighteenth-century instrument for which later composers have occasionally written. The size of a treble viol, it tended in shape toward highly fantastic contours. Usually it had 7 bowed strings, but behind these were 7 to 14 additional sympathetic strings made from thin wire which produced a silvery resonance.

The *lute* was the chief home-music instrument all over Europe in the sixteenth century. It was a plucked-string instrument with a round body in the shape of a halved pear, with a flat neck, fretted, and with a pegbox bent back at an angle. It normally had 11 strings, 5 of them tuned in octave or unison with the others, to be plucked simultaneously with them. The lute family includes the *mandolin*. The *guitar* family differs from the lute in that its members, except for the *cittern*, have flat backs. The sides of the guitar itself curve inward like those of the viols. The guitar superseded the lute in Spain, and later in France.

3. "Baroque," a term borrowed from the history of architecture, is commonly used to refer to music written between (approximately) 1600 and 1750.

A *clavier* is any stringed keyboard instrument. There are two large classes of claviers, those in which the mechanism causes a hammer to strike the string and those in which the mechanism causes a quill, or plectrum, to pluck the string. The former class originated in the *dulcimer* and came to include the *clavichord* and the modern *pianoforte;* the latter class originated in the *psaltery* and came to include *harpsichord*, *clavicembalo* (*cembalo*), *clavecin*, *virginal*, and *spinet* (all more or less synonymous, what differences there are depending largely on shape of box). The *harpsichord* proper is similar in shape to the grand piano. In modern examples there are often at least four strings to each key, which produce higher and lower octaves. Each key is connected with plectrums made of more than one material or placed so as to pluck the string nearer to or farther from the bridge, so that subtle differences in timbre are possible. This complicated apparatus is controlled by two manuals (keyboards) and by several pedal-couplers. Variations in volume as well as in timbre, blocked out as phrasal units, are thus made possible. Crescendo and diminuendo are, however, almost impossible. The harpsichord was the chief keyboard instrument of the Baroque period. It was the harpsichord's function to realize the thorough-bass accompaniment (also known as figured bass, basso continuo, or merely continuo—the bass "continuing through" the piece). Guided by numerical symbols entered beneath the bass part, the harpsichordist filled in the harmonic structure between bass and melody. This practice would seem to call for simple homophony, but harpsichordists became skilled in improvising a real contrapuntal structure over the thorough-bass. Cello or gamba doubled with harpsichord to reinforce the bass-line proper.

The *recorder* is an end-blown flute with a whistle mouthpiece. A complete family of recorders, from treble to bass, played an important part in domestic music of the sixteenth century (late Renaissance).

These are instruments of the past. What of instruments of the future? Electronic instruments are still young. None is as yet a member in good standing of the symphony orchestra. There has been a conservatism not only in the orchestra but in the new instruments themselves.

One or two interesting instruments have enabled the performer to seem to evoke and change musical tone with a mere wave of the hand, but, by and large, so far as the performer is concerned, present electronic instruments call for the same kinds of manipulation as acoustic instruments—keyboards, pedals, stops, strings to be fingered and bowed or plucked (there are few electronic instruments to blow like wind instruments, however). And the sounds which are produced by the new instruments have been too slavishly related to the sounds of traditional instruments. More volume, more sustaining power if the acoustic counterparts involve striking or plucking, control over the natural and unavoidable percussiveness of almost all our acoustic methods of setting a vibration going or changing a pitch, a new compactness and portability in organ-tone or bell-tone instruments—these have been the goals and the achievements of electronic instruments to date, plus a multiplication of the variety of sounds which any two hands or ten fingers can produce and a certain intermingling of species, as in pianos which can be themselves and can also imitate violin timbre and clarinet timbre. Between performer and the ultimate sound, all of course is different, not only the appearance of the instrument but its physics as well. Electrostatistically, electromagnetically, or photoelectrically, the sound of vibrating string or column of air may be changed into electricity or light, amplified, and then changed back into sound. Meanwhile, its harmonics have been knocked about, if a change in timbre was desired, and its duration has been extended. Or there may be no vibrating string or column, no sound in the first place; the whole process, from the beginning up to the point at which the end product comes out as sound, may be electrical. All this is new—the physics, that is—but the result has been old, the end-product is an imitation. Most unnecessarily so, for the sheer mathematical possibilities of the timbres that can be produced by electrical tinkering with harmonics are inexhaustible. New sounds, new timbres, new blends of timbre, a new massed sound—a single keyboard, perhaps, astonishing us not by its reproduction of the sound of a symphony orchestra but by its invention of a new "orchestra," whose sound, both in its individual components and in its ensemble, has never been heard and can therefore not at present be imagined—this is what the future should hold, though a century of trial and error may be necessary before the sound is one we want to hear.

6. STYLE

In our previous comparative discussion of a Bach fugue and a Beethoven slow movement, we pointed out some of the differences between the two works, although we emphasized the similarities. It was those similarities which brought out most clearly our concern of the moment, namely, the importance of paying attention to the specific behavior of the various passages within a given work. Let us now revert to some of the differences and, instead of regarding them only as differences between individual works—important as such differences are— think of them as evidence of different beliefs and desires—different purposes—in the minds of their composers. For every composer is, whether consciously or unconsciously, after something positive in his music; he has ideals of what music should be, and these ideals are among the controlling forces in his imagination.

Let us for a moment see what might be the result of looking at the same differences negatively. One might say that Beethoven's piece, compared with Bach's, lacks continuity. One might say the same thing of the Mozart minuet from K.387. Such a statement would, to be sure, have to be made in ignorance of the large-scale coherence of the music—its logic—but it has a certain plausibility. Or one might say that Bach's piece, compared with Beethoven's or with Mozart's, lacks contrast. Such a statement would betray an insensitivity to the subtlety of Bach's sense of contrast, but it, too, has a certain plausibility. Unfortunately, it is an easy step from statements such as these to dangerous judgments such as that Bach was incapable of dramatic surprise or that Beethoven and Mozart were unable to sustain a single mood. It is easy to demonstrate the falsity of these statements, since examples of their contraries are plentiful among the works of each composer.[1] But one never really wins an argument with a person offering such judgments, however strong one's case, because one's opponent has not been looking for what the composer was looking for. He has not tried to understand the composer's style.

If, then, we look positively at the differences between the Bach and the Beethoven and Mozart pieces, we may use them—and other works of the same composers—as evidence of divergent musical aims and ideals and as examples of the technical means used to realize them. These aims, ideals, and means are all aspects of style. Style is not only in how a piece sounds ("This sounds like Mozart"); it is also in how, to the mind of the composer, a piece ought to sound. The most important aspects of a style are those features of it which a composer takes for granted. These are the "norms" of the style. We may say, for instance, that among Bach's beliefs is a conviction that a piece of music normally intensifies a single mood and that among Beethoven's beliefs is a conviction that a piece of music is normally dramatic.

Keeping this in mind, it is not peculiar that Chopin, two of whose pieces we discussed earlier, was a great admirer of Bach but thought little of Beethoven. For Chopin, also, as those pieces show, loved a style which inculcated single moods. It is interesting that he admired the Piano Sonata in C-Sharp Minor of Beethoven (called, but not by the composer, the "Moonlight Sonata"), when we reflect that the opening movement has a strong family resemblance to certain Nocturnes of Chopin. The middle movement is in mood not unlike some of the passages in Chopin's Scherzos, and the finale has a certain *furioso* character found in many of Chopin's more violent moments. Similarity of purpose leads to admiration. Among the beliefs of all the composers we have studied in detail (Bach, Beethoven, Mozart, and Chopin) is one (probably not consciously held by any of them, so much was it taken for granted) that music is normally tonal. Each composer writes occasional passages in which tonality is weakened, even destroyed, but each always reverts to a strong feeling of key.

It has been possible so far in our discussion of music in this book to ignore style, for a simple reason: the examples used have all been taken from that

1. For example, the reader might play Bach's Fantasy in G Minor for organ, which juxtaposes conflicting moods, abounds in unexpected harmonic progressions, and, in itself, stands in dramatic contrast with the quite homogeneous fugue which follows it; or he might play the slow movement of Beethoven's *Sixth Symphony*, an extended piece in which the composer's subtle variety is fully matched by the singleness with which his effect is sustained.

shifting group of pieces known as the "standard repertory." Either they, or, at least, pieces in the same style, have been in varying degrees familiar from childhood to every person brought up in the Western tradition. Their styles do not seem exotic or otherwise obtrusive. They sound, in one way or another, as we have been conditioned to believe that music should sound. For that reason, it has been possible to discuss them without having first to clear away difficulties raised by style. And it has been important to do this because if, when one begins the study of music, one becomes too soon attracted to matters of style, one runs the serious risk of misjudging its importance and of considering knowledge of style to be an end in itself. It happens to be almost fatally easy for a person interested in music to learn to identify various styles, so that, confronted with a work which he has not heard before, he can name its composer with reasonable certainty, just as one can readily come to the point of ticking off painters' names in an unfamiliar gallery.

A style is a set of norms and a group of possibilities through a knowledge of which we are able to hear a piece of music in that style. A feeling for style is essential to musical understanding; it has as a by-product the ability to identify and label styles; but that ability is not an end in itself. The end is musical understanding.

A composer evolves his own style out of those qualities in his musical experience with which his character is most sympathetic. As we have seen, style includes both techniques and ideals. A composer's training—both his formal training as a pupil and his lifelong study of other people's music—will inevitably affect the way in which he imagines his own music, but it is clear that the energy he gives to the music of others will be given largely to those works which exemplify principles and practices which he is ready to admire and which, to him, are rich in suggestion. Music, like language, is not invented out of whole cloth; it cannot be, if it is to have meaning.

It is impossible fully to describe a style, for it is a configuration of elements such that the whole is more than a sum of its parts. But it is possible, by comparison and contrast, so to separate styles as to enhance one's awareness of their peculiar individualities. And it is also possible to detect the sympathies between one composer and certain of his predecessors and so to find fruitful points of departure for the understanding of his music.

We shall conclude our consideration of music in this book with some comparisons between the music of Stravinsky and that of certain of his predecessors. This is not by any means an exhaustive study; it is intended to be suggestive of the value inherent in the thoughtful comparison of styles.

One of the most influential stylistic tendencies in European music in the late nineteenth century (and continuing into the early twentieth) is usually referred to as *nationalism.*

Musical nationalism (which was, in most countries, pleasantly unconnected with chauvinism) has two aspects which, though found together on occasion, are not necessarily present in the same work. In operas, tone poems, and other pieces of music with extra-musical (usually literary) components, the use of episodes from national history, of materials from national epics or traditional tales, and of symbolic embodiments of national character are all referred to as examples of nationalism.[2] More important as an influence upon the subsequent history of music is the other aspect of musical nationalism: the borrowing, as thematic material, of the traditional melodies (songs and dances) of one's own country or the invention of melodies in that style. This kind of nationalism was more common in countries relatively new to the musical scene (such as Russia and Bohemia) or in countries which had, in the past, played a prominent part in the history of music but which had been relatively unproductive for a good many years (such as England and Spain). In both kinds of nationalism there is, either latent or overt, a mystical approach to an ideal national character, conceived of as a continuing particular genius inherent in an ethnic group rather than in individuals. A certain kind of tune is thought of as being, let us say, peculiarly Russian; another as being peculiarly Spanish, and so on. And, indeed, these national characters are usually quite readily recognizable. An important feature of this tendency is that many composers were almost as much interested in the traditional music and the indigenous atmosphere of other countries as they were in those of their own. The exotic had almost as strong a claim as the native. In Russia, composers were especially fond of creating an oriental atmosphere by means of evocative tone-colors and the use of Near-Eastern scales. Rimsky-Korsakov's *Coq d'or,* for example, is lavish in its orientalism.

Russian musical nationalism in particular was an extensive movement, very

2. E.g., Tchaikovsky's "1812 Overture" is a tone poem based on Napoleon's ill-fated invasion of Russia; Wagner's *Ring of the Nibelung* is a series of operas (music dramas) making use of the *Nibelungenlied* and of Norse mythology; Sibelius' "Finlandia" embodies a national anthem without words, so to speak.

impressive abroad, and important in the formation of Stravinsky's imagination. A comparison between some of its characteristic features and those of certain late-nineteenth-century German music may serve to illuminate the whole problem of style.[3]

We have seen that in much of the music we have considered so far there is a differentiation according to function among the various passages in a work. We have spoken, for instance, of modulatory passages and of developments. We may also observe that in the main stream of European music in the eighteenth and nineteenth centuries (in Germany, France, and Italy) there is a preference for and a widespread use of various relatively complex compositional procedures, such as, for example, sonata form, rondo, and fugue. Each of these procedures implies variety of function in its passages. Each is, in large measure, a means of developing musical ideas. In the course of time, these procedures, and others related to them, came to be thought of primarily as such means. Contemporary admirers of Brahms, for instance, were particularly fond of his developments. And contemporary admirers of Wagner, too (not always, by any means, the same persons), praised the symphonic developments of his dramatic works. The use of musical material, especially when its mood was transformed during development, was at least as important as the material itself.

The Russian nationalists, on the other hand, tended to put all their eggs in the basket of the immediate effectiveness of their themes. In their most characteristic moments they did not manipulate; they stated and restated, with varied and colorful repetitions supported by individualized accompaniments.

3. The reader is advised to familiarize himself with the repertory of pieces which will be referred to by way of illustration in the ensuing discussion. This repertory is as follows:

BACH: *Brandenburg Concerto No. 3, in G Major.*
BERG: *Sonata for Piano.*
BRAHMS: *Variations on a Theme by Haydn; Symphony No. 3* (third movement).
DEBUSSY: "Prélude à l'après-midi d'un faun"; "La mer"; *Pelléas et Mélisande* (love scene in Act IV , scene 4); "La terrasse aux audiences du clair de lune"; "La fille aux cheveux de lin."
FRANCK: *Symphony.*
MOUSSORGSKY: *Pictures at an Exhibition;* Prelude to *Khovantchina; Boris Godunov* ("Coronation Scene" and "Idiot's Song").
MOZART: *Le Nozze di Figaro* (general reference).
RAVEL: *Rapsodie espagnole; Sonatine* for piano.
RIMSKY-KORSAKOV: *Capriccio espagnol; Shéhérazade; Le coq d'or* (selections will suffice).
STRAVINSKY: *Firebird Suite; Le sacre du printemps; Pétrouchka; L'histoire du soldat; Sérénade en la* for piano; *Symphonie de psaumes; Concerto in E flat* ("Dumbarton Oaks"); *Mass; The Rake's Progress.*
WAGNER: *Tristan und Isolde* (Prelude, "Love-Death," and love scene in Act II; *Die Meistersinger von Nürnberg* (Quintet in Act III, and the passage leading up to it).

They did not prepare, modulate, and develop. They relied on their thematic invention. They could afford to do so because they favored complete tunes, full-fledged themes, rather than passages developed out of motives. A comparison between the "Love-Death" from Wagner's *Tristan und Isolde* and the "Variations" in Rimsky-Korsakov's *Capriccio espagnol* will make this difference clear. The Wagner is constantly moving some place; it has a "seeking" effect. It relies heavily on the sequential development of motives and is almost always modulating. The Rimsky-Korsakov has several individualized variations—individualized in tone-color, in kind of accompaniment, and in rhythm. Different keys are used, but there are no modulatory passages between them—they are simply contrasted. Perhaps it would be helpful to say that the Wagner is always going somewhere and the Rimsky always is somewhere. One cannot pick out a separate, self-contained tune from the Wagner; it is all one long melody (what the composer called "eine ewige Melodie"); each variation in the Rimsky is a complete tune, and it is obvious that the tunes are closely related; we are plainly hearing the same tune in different versions. In a work such as Brahms's *Variations on a Theme by Haydn*, we hear, instead, a series of pieces with several features in common, but certainly not several versions of the original tune. The difference is important; in the Rimsky, the listener is not puzzled by the connection between one variation and the next—it is so clear that he can abandon himself to the immediate pleasures of the new color, the new rhythm, the new accompaniment; in the Brahms, the similarities in form and in general melodic outlines and harmonic progressions, and the varieties of variation within those similarities, make a work which depends far more on memory, on expectation, and on the course of the whole. Put in another way, the music of Brahms and Wagner lives far more in long-range effects than does a work like *Capriccio espagnol*.

The Russian nationalists cultivated pure tone-color far more than did the German romantics. That is, they favored the particular sounds of individual instruments over the more general sound of an orchestration with much doubling.[4] There are a great many full-dress solos in this music. Note, for instance, the cadenzas[5] for various instruments which introduce the "Gypsy Dance" in *Capriccio espagnol*. Or the oboe solos in the *Khovantchina* Prelude. Not only are

4. "Doubling" in orchestration means that the various lines of the texture are each played by combinations of instruments with differing tone-colors, so that no one color clearly predominates.

5. Improvisatory solo passages, usually unaccompanied.

melodies individualized in color; accompaniments are as well. The "Gypsy Dance" is characteristic in its accompaniments; they are almost as attractive to the ear as the tune itself. The rhythms are lively and distinct; the colors are bright; there is an air of clarity and vitality. No one else uses the percussion instruments so lavishly—or so cannily—as the Russian nationalist.

These technical features reflect serious differences in purpose. In a work such as Berg's *Sonata for Piano*, for instance, we feel an overwhelming personal importance. The music seems to arise out of the very self of the composer, and one cannot listen sympathetically to it without becoming intimately involved in it. One does not observe the music; it takes one by the lapel. Music such as the Prelude to *Tristan* does not depict or symbolize as in a spectacle the unsatisfied longing of the lovers on the stage: it engulfs the audience in its inexorable, surging chromaticism. The Russian nationalists are more objective, presentational, spectacular. They may overwhelm by hieratic mass effects as in the "Coronation Scene" in Moussorgsky's *Boris Godunov* (or listen to the "bell" variation in the *Khovantchina* Prelude), but one is not invited into an inner sanctum; their music is too folksy, too public, to be so personal.

One will go astray if one supposes that the tendencies we have been describing are the exclusive tendencies in the works of those composers whom we have mentioned. The German romantics have their simple moments; in fact, those moments, frequent in songs and short pieces, are among their best. And Rimsky-Korsakov, who was a highly trained composer (most of the Russian nationalists were amateurs), was quite at home in the symphonic style. There is, for instance, the famous *Shéhérazade*. But we are quite safe in saying that the tendencies we have been describing are the leading ones in each case, especially if we sum up the differences in ideal of musical continuity. The preference in the late-nineteenth-century symphonic style, especially in Germany, is for a continuity in which every musical idea within a movement either should appear to be evolved out of its predecessor or, if it is introduced (as it frequently is) by way of strong contrast, should have its connection with the other material demonstrated later in the piece; in the Russian nationalists, extreme clarity of form, expressed in sharply defined sections and in the avoidance of every kind of non-theme-stating passage except for introductions, cadenzas, and brief codas, is sought for and obtained. Perhaps the most convincing demonstration of this important difference would result from comparing two pieces the general procedures of which are such that one might well expect the opposite. In Moussorgsky's *Pictures at an Exhibition* (either in the original piano piece or in Ravel's masterly version of it for orchestra) the program includes the notion of walking through a gallery from picture to picture, and this walking is symbolized by a recurring tune. It would be quite in order for one "picture" to fade out and gradually give way to the next; notice, however, that even in those cases in which the opening of the new "picture" is anticipated during the "walk," it is quite clear at what point the new piece begins; there is no formal vagueness. In the third movement of his *Symphony No. 3, in F Major,* Brahms makes use of one of his favorite procedures, the *A B A*. This procedure by nature involves contrast, and contrast between *A* and *B* is striking. But Brahms then proceeds to connect his two themes: the return to *A* is carefully prepared while *B* is dying out; and, in the coda, the opening of *B* is inextricably woven into a melody which is an extension of *A*. Wagner was particularly proud (and justifiably so) of his mastery of "the art of transition," the art of moving from one section to another in such a way that the material of the first appears to be transformed into that of the second. A beautiful example can be found in the passage leading up to the quintet in Act III of *Die Meistersinger*. Moussorgsky, had he been given, as Wagner was, to public confession, would probably rather have pointed with pride to the many fruits of his enviable melodic invention, such as the "Idiot's Song" at the end of *Boris Godunov*. It is, after all, a considerable feat to have rivaled the beauty of such traditional melodies as those with which we began our discussion, the "Londonderry Air" and "Adeste Fideles."

The deliberate drive toward overt unity so characteristic of late romanticism (in both France and Germany) extended to works in several movements, such as symphonies. In a so-called "cyclical" symphony, such as the great symphony by Franck, there are thematic cross-references among the movements; and the finale synthesizes all the main ideas into one statement. The same preoccupation is expressed by Wagner's recurrent use of a small group of incisive themes ("leading motives") throughout an entire opera.

In some respects, those French composers who struck out on new paths—especially Debussy and Ravel—resemble the Russian nationalists; in others, they are more like the romantic symphonists. Much as they admired the Russians—Moussorgsky in particular—it would be impossible for them to be in complete sympathy with them. Essential to the Russians' success was the fact that most of them were amateurs and could therefore more readily take a really fresh view. But French music has the longest continuous tradition in Europe, and in no other country is a composer more thoroughly trained in his craft. Debussy may well have been the most radical composer of the last hundred years, but neither by training nor by temperament could he have had any but the most painstaking attitude toward the art of composition.[6]

In a work such as Debussy's "Prélude à l'après-midi d'un faun," melodies, as in Wagner, grow out of clearly defined motives; the art of transition, resulting in an air of brilliant improvisation, is as great as in Brahms and, if possible, more subtle. But there is unquestionably greater objectivity; climaxes are less personal and direct: in a work such as *La mer*, they may overwhelm by their grandeur, but they remain impersonal. What we called above "personal importance," the French felt strongly was pomposity and pretentiousness. They favored modesty, not because of a lack of will to expressiveness, but because they felt more effect was possible with a less hectic general level. It would be instructive to compare the point of greatest lyric intensity in the love scene in *Pelléas et Mélisande* ("Toutes les étoiles tombent") with a moment of relative calm in the corresponding scene in *Tristan und Isolde*, such as the passage beginning "Das süsse Wörtlein 'und.'" Great circumspectness in the use of the sequence, rather than the almost constant use of it for its tendency to produce climaxes, is an important technical feature of this French style. One might compare what happens to motives in "L'après-midi" with what happens to them in Berg's *Sonata*.

The similarity between this French music and that of the Russian nationalists is particularly striking in color and in rhythm. A work such as Ravel's *Rapsodie espagnole* makes this quite clear. But the same work makes just as clear that the view of melody and of texture is radically different. In the "Prélude à la nuit," for example, a melody is hinted at rather than stated. In general, in the works of both Debussy and Ravel there can be, paradoxically, particular clarity of melodic motive along with suggestive vagueness of melody. In Debussy's "Terrasse aux audiences du clair de lune," for instance, the motives are clearly distinct, but one feels curiously unable quite to overhear the melodies into which they grow. And this atmospheric quality is frequently promoted by a vagueness of texture—a genuine background; the melody rests on a mattress of sound, so

6. The professional Rimsky-Korsakov felt obliged to polish—in some cases to orchestrate from piano sketches—the works of more than one of his extraordinarily gifted but amateur colleagues.

to speak, or is surrounded by a halo. There is a great difference between this kind of effect and the clear brilliance so frequent in Russian accompaniments. Again, one should not overlook other, opposing qualities in the music: the clear tunefulness of a piece such as Debussy's "La fille aux cheveux de lin," or the hard and definite texture of a movement such as the finale of Ravel's piano *Sonatine*.

If, now, we turn to a fairly early piece by Stravinsky, the *Firebird Suite*, we find the expression of many sympathies with both the Russian and the French tendencies we have been observing. The piece is very Russian in its color, its rhythm, its melody, its clarity of form, and its program, and it marks the beginning of Stravinsky's long and fruitful association with the ballet. The massive folk-song finale (not at all unlike the "Coronation Scene" in *Boris Godunov*) is peculiarly Russian. In the very opening, however, we also see an affinity with the French in the suggestive and atmospheric orchestral effects and the fragmented melody.

If we keep in mind the Russians' fondness for clear sectionalism as a key formal procedure, and their feeling for the vital importance of impressive accompaniment, we can see that in a somewhat later work, *Le sacre du printemps*, the general procedure is still the same. The texture has become more complex, but the relationship between melody and accompaniment, the melodic type, and the brilliance of color are still distinctly Russian, although the melodies tend to separate into individualized motives and the line may be almost evanescent. And the same thing may be said of *Pétrouchka*. The *Sacre du printemps* and *Pétrouchka*, using the same procedures yet sounding so divergent, together provide a convincing demonstration, if one is needed, of the fact that the significance of procedures is not that they provide means of classification; they are, rather, means toward the apprehension of the unique progress of the individual work.

In the works of Stravinsky written during the last thirty years or so we can detect certain features which have enriched and modified, though not denatured, his style.

The historical labors of nineteenth-century musicians and musical scholars—labors still being pursued in our time—have had strong influences upon the composers of recent generations. In the past, musical activity had revolved almost entirely about contemporary music. There were, to be sure, the traditional repertories of religious music and of popular song and dance; but novelty, firmly rooted in the immediate past, was, in general, more sought after than the preservation of some constant, "classical" repertory. In the musical life of the present not only is there a "standard repertory" but that repertory is being constantly widened by the inclusion of music from all times in Western history. There is now a greater consciousness than ever before of the stylistic variety of our music, as more and more of it becomes available. The advantage is obvious in the enrichment of our musical possibilities. The disadvantages, however, although they are less obvious, are at least as great. Styles have to be learned by audiences, and much more learning is asked of the present-day audience than was asked of any in the past. This learning, when effective, is in the form of habitual responses acquired through attentive listening to many performances. It is no wonder that the audience is often reluctant to be hospitable to new music. There has always been some such reluctance (on occasion, it has been expressed with considerable violence), but it is particularly acute today.

The composer, although he has more difficulty in gaining a sympathetic hearing, has, as a member of the audience himself, a wider range of stylistic experience, and the relationships between his music and that of others are likely to be more extended in time and place than ever before. Historical studies and the cultivation of folk music by the nationalists coincided in one respect: they led to a widespread revival of diatonic modes other than the major and minor. The folk songs of most countries, along with most of the art music written before about 1600, make use of far more modes than the two which are familiar from the developments of the last three hundred years. These older modes opened up many possibilities for the refreshment of diatonic harmony. Their presence also encouraged the invention of new modes, such as the whole-tone scale.[7]

The music of the past has been particularly rich in suggestions to Stravinsky. For instance, the *Concerto in E flat* ("Dumbarton Oaks") makes use of procedures intimately allied with those of the early-eighteenth-century concerto grosso. The first movement even begins with a rhythmic figure quite commonly used in the eighteenth century: for example, in the first movement of Bach's *Brandenburg Concerto No. 3, in G Major*. The opera, *The Rake's Progress*, has considerable affinity, especially in the operatic ideals it embodies, with the Italian opera of the late eighteenth and early nineteenth centuries. To get at the importance of this affinity, compare *The Rake's Progress* with an opera such as

7. The commonest of the modes mentioned here may be found on pp. 127–28.

Mozart's *Le Nozze di Figaro* and then with Wagner's *Tristan und Isolde*. Many persons have found that an acquaintance with Gregorian chant and with sacred music of the fourteenth and fifteenth centuries is helpful in hearing the *Mass*.[8] Examples could be multiplied. All would serve to illustrate Stravinsky's individuality, however; he is not a man of many styles but a man of wide sympathies.

The coincidence of the economic strictures resulting from World War I with the esthetic convictions of Stravinsky had a refining influence upon his music. His media tend to be modest in size—his outlook restrained.

An extreme case is that of *L'histoire du soldat*, in which the variety of a full orchestra is suggested in a small group by reducing the wood winds to clarinet and bassoon, the brass to cornet and trombone, the strings to a single violin and a single double-bass, and the percussion to one player who, however, has to be an acrobat to manage all the instruments assigned to him.

Stravinsky has expressed his creed and described his methods in a set of lectures printed as *The Poetics of Music*. From this book we are confirmed in the belief we already had from hearing the music that Stravinsky's idea of music is that it has life and meaning of its own; not that it is a form of personal diary. Stravinsky, a profoundly religious man, believes that music comes from God and that it has the religious mission of helping to establish a communion among men. In this, he reminds one of Haydn, and, like Haydn—indeed, like most profoundly religious men—he has a gift for the comic and the satiric. There are, for example, the parodies of popular dances in *L'histoire du soldat*. The seriousness of a Wagner is one that includes taking one's self at least as seriously as one's works; it implies the attempt to translate one's better moments into sound; the seriousness of a Stravinsky or a Haydn is centered on an ideal of perfection in the making of the work itself, be the mood of that work light or heavy. This is not by any means to imply that Wagner was not a serious workman; he was. But his overriding ambition was for each of his works to have a world-shaking significance. And it was this air of importance, combined with the almost incredible magic of Wagner's music, which, through the reaction against it, reinforced that attitude of restraint, modesty, and sobriety which is characteristic of so much modern musical thinking, including that of Stravinsky.

8. Good recordings of Gregorian melodies are readily available. Unfortunately the same cannot be said, as yet, of the other music referred to. Machaut's *Mass* would make a particularly helpful comparison.

In spite of the multiplicity of stylistic resonances in Stravinsky's music, he has certain cardinal procedures that are constant. One is a personal kind of tonality which is compatible with older tonalities in that it allows using them but which is, nevertheless, different in an important respect. In the works of Bach or of Beethoven, for instance, a tonic is a single keynote upon which a triad is built. This triad may be disposed in any way suitable to the progress of the particular piece; in any one of several possible forms it can have the significance of a point of departure or of repose. In Stravinsky's music, points of departure and points of repose tend to be quite specific chords—combinations of tones regarded not as disposable in various ways but as individual sonorities. There may be two or more such sonorities in a Stravinsky movement. The harmony moves among them as among poles of attraction. Even the slightest changes in them tell heavily. They may among themselves demand yet another sonority as a point of rest—as in the movements of the *Sérénade en la* for piano, all of which end on un-harmonized *A*'s—or they may not. Each piece has its own tonality.

For example, in the third movement of the *Symphonie de psaumes*, the first harmonies impinge on the particular sonority reached on the last syllable of the word "Alleluia." This sonority is the basis of the setting of the next word, "Laudate," during which it is altered so as to impinge on the sonority used to set the word "Dominum." In the following passage there is a most telling effect achieved by playing with small changes in this sonority. Just before the allegro part, a single new tone added to the "Dominum" chord makes it into a point of departure for the harmonic movement of that part. And so on, throughout the movement. There is a tendency for any one passage to remain relatively static about a pole of sonority and for movement to be from one such relatively static place to another.

This feature is allied with a peculiarity of many of Stravinsky's melodies—a peculiarity with a solid ancestry in Russian traditional song and dance, but strongly influenced by the motivic character of late-nineteenth-century French music. These melodies move about with varying stresses and slight changes of order among a small group of notes. It is easy to see how this fits in with the notion of specific, subtly varied, sonorities. Passages quite diverse in effect may well have this feature in common. For instance, the beginning of the second part of the *Sacre*, the section called "Pagan Night," is built upon a sonority far thicker than any one would be likely to find in a later work. The harmony pulses about this polar sonority. This background, with its ostinato[9] rhythm, has the same function as, for example, the accompaniments in the "Gypsy" movement of the *Capriccio espagnol*. Above it is a very fragmentary melody, which does not appear immediately, built on only four different pitches. And the same kind of intense lyricism can be found in the fugue subject which opens the second movement of the *Symphonie de psaumes*.

There is an equally characteristic view of measure in this music. The feeling of steady pulses is usually more important here than any feeling of meter in establishing rhythmic continuity. Stravinsky desires the listener to be conscious in his music of the steady flow of time. The eye of a person looking at a Stravinsky score is far more likely to be startled by the frequent changes of metrical signs than is the ear of a person listening to the same piece, so firm is the pulse as a basis for the rhythmic variety above it.

Harmony, melody, and rhythm tend together to establish a powerful homogeneity in any one passage in a Stravinsky work. But the clear separation of passages is as vital in this music as it is in that of the Russian nationalists. There, varied repetition, or sharp alternation of diverse materials, was the norm. Here, however, the most simple view of many pieces would symbolize their formal procedure as *A B C D*, etc. Each piece has its own kind of movement within this general procedure, which is no more in itself a prescription of movement than is our old friend *A B A*.[10] For example, in the "Dumbarton Oaks" concerto, the final passage in the first movement constitutes a clarification of the opening passage; the same thing is true of the far more varied third movement. And the three movements of that work—movements which have no thematic material in common—are bound together by means of a slow transition from the first movement to the second, referred to briefly in the middle of the second movement, which recurs in varied form between the second and the third. It is characteristic that this transition has nothing about it of the "art of transition"; it is, rather, quite clearly separated from its surroundings in tempo, color, and motive. But one cannot expect these particular procedures to be followed in other works. The finale of the *Symphonie de psaumes*, for instance, is quite different. It has a

9. Literally, "obstinate," that is, frequently repeated.

10. To take two pieces which have already been discussed, compare the Mozart minuet from the G-Major Quartet, K.387, with the third movement of Brahms's *Third Symphony*. Both are *A B A* pieces. The Mozart makes a point of leaving the contrast between the two sections sharp. The Brahms makes the quite different point of first displaying the contrast and then eliminating it.

refrain, and a large portion of its allegro is repeated (with changes) later in the movement, but—and this is true of all Stravinsky's more extended movements— it is in the harmonic and melodic progress from one section to the next and in the demands that must be satisfied by the implication of that progress, that the key to the movement lies. The sound of the music is Stravinsky's, but the way in which we listen is the same as the way in which we listened earlier to the Bach and Beethoven pieces. For we hear *through* style and *through* our knowledge of general procedures.

Slowly, as we build up our knowledge of various styles in the form of habitual expectations, we are able more fully to respond to music in those styles. Our response to the *fortissimo* passage we discussed in the Beethoven adagio is far greater if we are aware of Beethoven's fondness for such startling effects, for we know that the possibility of them always hangs over his quiet pieces and makes their calm precarious. Our amazement at the choral outburst which interrupts the aria in Handel's *Messiah* which we described is far keener if we are aware of the extreme abnormality of texture at that point: Handel's choruses do not normally begin without harmonized accompaniment unless they are fugues. Our feeling for the third (and final) section of the middle movement of the "Dumbarton Oaks" concerto is far truer if we are aware of Stravinsky's preoccupation with the ballet—aware, that is, from listening to his music rather than from simply being told about it. In fact, all we have been doing in this book is giving examples of a way in which to build up, from intensive listening, habitual responses to individual works. All music is movement. We follow that movement and respond to the expectations, disappointments, delays, and fulfilments aroused by it, through memory, through knowledge of musical procedures, and through a feeling for style—a feeling which is at its best when it has become instinctive. Each work is an individual experience with its own peculiar expression. Our aim is to hear it as directly as possible.

CONSTRUCTIVE ELEMENTS

7. COMMON PROCEDURES AND TYPES

In the following pages are listed and described (1) the formal procedures most widely used in the repertory which one normally encounters in present-day performances, (2) those names of single pieces or of individual movements in that repertory which are such as to give a clue to the kind of formal procedure one may expect to find followed in them, (3) the commonest compound types (pieces in more than one movement) in the repertory, (4) some of the peculiarities of music which is strongly influenced by extra-musical considerations.

The time space covered is from the late seventeenth century to the present, although certain kinds of sixteenth-century music are described. Even within these limitations, the list does not pretend to the completeness of standard reference works such as *The Harvard Dictionary of Music* or *Grove's Dictionary of Music and Musicians*, works to which the reader is referred for information not found in these pages.

PROCEDURES

The term *binary* refers to two closely related procedures. One has been described in the body of this book as the antecedent-consequent procedure. The other falls into two parts or sections, each of which is repeated. The graphic representation of this would be $|:A:\||:B:\|$. Similar musical material is employed in both sections, which are further bound together by a system of complementary modulations. Ordinarily the first section begins in the tonic and moves to the dominant key, and the second section starts from the dominant and works back to the tonic. In minor the modulation is to the relative major key and back again

101

(for example, A minor—C major—A minor). The two sections in binary form may or may not be of equal length, and, if they differ, the second is always longer than the first. The name "rounded binary" has been given to a common variant of the form. Frequently the *A* section is repeated either in whole or in part after the *B* section, so that in graphic representation the plan becomes $|:A:\|:BA:\|$.

One of the most astonishing things in the history of music is the emergence in the late eighteenth century of complex and relatively long pieces in the rounded binary form. This form had existed for a long time in short pieces, such as dances, but during the late eighteenth century it grew tremendously and became what is now known as the *sonata form*. The expansion was accomplished by linking together and packing into an "exposition" a far greater amount of musical material than is normally found in part *A* of a dance. And the expansion of part *A* led to a proportional expansion of the other parts. The sonata form makes dramatic use of the principle of contrast: contrast of keys, of themes, and of textures—contrast in dynamics and in timbre.

For the sonata as a whole and the various sonata types (the string quartet, the symphony, the concerto, etc.) the reader should refer to the section "Compound Types" below. *Sonata form* is the term applied to the characteristic structure of a single movement or of single movements within a sonata but not to the sonata as a whole. Other terms in common use are "sonata-allegro form" and "first-movement form," neither of which is entirely satisfactory, since sonata form is sometimes the structure of *slow* movements which are not *first* movements. We shall give here only the essential outlines of sonata form as exhibited in works of the classical or late-eighteenth-century period. Below are listed the structural features which the majority of sonata-form movements of this period have in common.

There may or may not be an *Introduction*

A *Exposition*—divided broadly into two parts:

> *Theme I*[1]—a theme or group of themes in the tonic key; there may or may not be a *bridge passage* during which a modulation takes place; a bridge passage may use material of its own or material previously introduced

1. The terms "Theme I" and "Theme II" are poor descriptions, but the literature on music uses them so frequently that avoiding them would probably lead to confusion. "Group I" and "Group II" would be more satisfactory terms.

Theme II—a theme or, more usually, a group of themes in a key related to the tonic key; the related key is commonly—though not necessarily—the *dominant* (if the tonic key is major) or the *relative major* (if the tonic key is minor); the last theme in the exposition is often called a *closing theme* or a *codetta*

A *Exposition* repeated

B *Development*—"working-out section" or "free fantasia"—modulatory in character—unfolding of previous material frequently leading to a climax—perhaps, however, introducing new material

A′ *Recapitulation*—restatement of the exposition with certain modifications
    Theme I in tonic key
    Bridge passage modified so as not to modulate to new key
    Theme II in tonic key

B *Development* repeated

A′ *Recapitulation* repeated

There may or may not be a *Coda*

The oldest examples of sonata form are in this expanded version of the rounded binary. However, the development section came to be so long, and often so climactic in character, that the form tended to drop the repetition of the development and recapitulation and thus became *A A B A′*. Still later, in many examples, the exposition is not repeated, and the form becomes *A B A′*. Of the three large sections, the first is characterized by duality, the second by diversity, and the third by unity of key.

One of the most common of all formal designs for short compositions— operatic arias in the eighteenth century, the minuet and trio of many sonatas, quartets, and symphonies, and most short piano pieces—is *ternary form (A B A)*, sometimes called "three-part song form." The first section of ternary form, unlike that of binary, usually closes in the tonic key and is in many cases self-contained and complete. And since the *B* section ordinarily introduces entirely new material in a different key, ternary form may be regarded as looser in structure than binary.

Ternary form exemplifies in embryo the principle of alternating sections used in another formal design—*rondo form*, which is often the form employed in the finales of sonatas, quarters, and concertos of the classical period. The essentials of rondo form are a main theme or "rondo" which recurs in alternation with contrasting sections called *episodes*. Two common variants of the form are: (1)

A B A C A and (2) *A B A C A B A*. The first of these is known as "short rondo form," the second as "rondo-sonata form." In both, *A* represents the main theme, while *B* and *C* are episodes. It is a principle of the form that each recurrence of the main theme should be in the tonic key, the episodes being in different keys. The rondo-sonata is basically a rondo with some features of sonata form. The main theme (*A*) and the first episode (*B*) assume the characteristic qualities of Themes I and II of a sonata-form movement. The central episode (*C*) is not always truly episodical (i.e., constructed out of new material); it often develops material from the earlier sections. The next *A* and *B* resemble a recapitulation. The final *A* is often expanded into a coda.

The procedures so far described depend upon the relationships among clearly defined phrases and groups of phrases, largely with respect to tonality. They are, as procedures, almost entirely independent of the obligation to use any specified amount of thematic material. But during the course of the nineteenth century they came more and more to be thought of in terms of contrasted, though interconnected, materials. The reader is also reminded that different procedures may be followed on different levels in a piece, as we saw earlier in discussing a Mozart minuet.

A piece which proceeds on the *ritornello* principle begins with a statement in the tonic key of the main thematic materials. This opening statement is called a *ritornello*. The rest of the piece consists of complete or partial restatements of the ritornello in various related keys, alternating with episodes tending to be sequential in character and based on material closely allied with, or actually taken from, that of the ritornello. An allied procedure is that of the recurrent *refrain*.

A work in *variation form* (*A A' A'' A'''*, etc.) consists of a simple, short theme and a set of different versions of that theme. Variations, to *be* variations, must be like the theme in some respects and different from it in others. They may, for example, retain the harmonic structure of the theme; they may retain both the harmonies and the melodic outline of the theme, in which case the melody is usually ornamented; they may alter the harmony of the theme while yet preserving the larger structural outlines of the theme—the number of measures and cadential endings; or the variations may be so free as to make even the structural outlines of the theme unrecognizable. There are many ways of varying a theme: change in melodic contour, in harmonic structure, in melodic and harmonic rhythm; alteration in form, texture, key, mode, meter, tempo—these may occur singly or in combination. A common procedure is to detach a melodic figure from the theme and to develop it throughout a variation. An independent figure, one not derived from the theme, may be similarly treated. In a work in this form, the variations are of course related not only to the theme but also to one another. Similarities and contrasts among variations should be noted and also the order and grouping of the variations.

The *theme with variations*, in earlier examples, tended to be very definitely divided into sections, each forming an apparently complete musical statement and ending on a full cadence followed by a split-second pause. But with and since Beethoven the theme with variations has come more and more to be a single indivisible entity, with the points of demarcation between sections blurred and without pause. For that matter, in the earliest theme with variations at least three-quarters of the significance of a variation is lost without its relation to the theme or comparison with the other variations, so that the type is basically single. In the history of the theme-with-variations type, structure (number of measures, arrangement of sections and phrases, cadential endings) has held out most stubbornly in resisting variation, harmonic scheme next, and melody (aside from its ornamentation, which was one of the first means of variation) next. But since Brahms even the structure of the theme has been swept away in the "free" variations, or "symphonic" variations, in which the essential melodic motive or motives of the theme are rhythmically "transformed" so as to have new characters, and each transformation becomes the basis of development in its own variation.

Two peculiar types of what are essentially "theme with variations" must be examined apart from the primary type. These are the *passacaglia* and the *chaconne*. Scholars have been cracking their skulls for a century trying to distinguish surely between them on the basis of the works which early composers have labeled with one or the other name. All that can be said with assurance is that composers of the period 1600–1750 used the two names indiscriminately. Both types were traditionally moderately slow in tempo, triple in meter; in both, the harmonic rhythm was slow, changing with each measure. Both were originally dances. Both are "continuous" variations, that is, there is no full cadence, no break marking off the sections. Moreover, strangely enough, they are without a "theme," if by theme one insists on meaning a melody. What takes the place of a theme in these types is either a "ground bass" (passacaglia?) or an absolutely fixed succession of chords (chaconne?). A ground bass, also called "basso ostinato" (obstinate bass), is a bass line of normally from 4 to 8 measures (the customary "theme" is anywhere from 16 to 48 measures, often being a full binary structure), repeated over and over again through the entire length of the work; occasionally it may be transferred to an upper voice.

Double is a name given in the eighteenth century to a simple type of variation consisting chiefly of the addition of embellishments.

Strophic form (*A A A*, etc.) is exemplified in those songs employing the same music for successive stanzas of a poetic text. Obviously, such a structure will hardly be found in instrumental music.

An *additive* form (*A B C D*, etc.) is often made possible and desirable in music which depends primarily for its coherence upon a text, as do most motets and many songs (see "Single Types" below). Otherwise, it must adhere in some manner to the principle of return (as brilliantly illustrated by the style of Stravinsky), or it will run the risk of degenerating into a potpourri.

Paradoxically, one of the most important procedures in music is the one of avoiding a procedure, of proceeding informally, as in a *fantasy*, in a *recitative*, or in many *slow introductions*. This procedure is characterized by free, often startling, modulation, passing from one key to another, from that key to still another, and so on, with the object of surprising and thus pleasing the listener. It capitalizes on the unexpected, both because the listener expects the unexpected and because the lack of a formal procedure makes any long-range expectation impossible. The main intention is either to reproduce the effect of an improvisation—hence a fondness for unestablished rhythms and fantastic contrasts of material—or, more commonly, to arouse the indefinite expectation that a passage or a movement of a formal nature is about to begin. Indeed, the procedure "unformed followed by formed" is one of the most valuable ones in music, e.g., recitative and aria (see "Single Types" below), slow introduction and sonata-form allegro, fantasy and fugue; and the alternation between "free" passages and more formal ones characterizes the eighteenth-century *toccata*.

The various formal procedures so far considered are all what might be called "sectional forms." The principles of organization exemplified in them are (1) repetition of clearly defined sections and (2) contrast between sections. We turn now to music of another sort, in which sectional procedure, though present, is less emphasized than is continuity of flow.

A *fugue* is a polyphonic imitative composition for instruments or singing voices or both, in a definite number of melodic parts, exposed and developed in a logical tonal order. The *exposition* of a fugue consists of successive announcements of a melodic phrase called the *subject* by each voice in turn. (The various melodic strands of a fugue are called "voices" whether they are sung or played.)

Below is an outline of the typical procedure followed in the exposition of a four-voice fugue. Since there is no fixed order of entry for the various voices, we shall assume the order to be soprano, alto, tenor, and bass.

1. *Subject* enunciated by soprano voice alone in tonic key
2. *Answer* given by alto voice in dominant key (the answer being the subject transposed and, usually, slightly altered); countersubject (or free counterpoint) in soprano; this may be followed by a short episode or codetta modulating back to the tonic key
3. *Subject* announced by tenor voice in tonic key; countersubject in alto; free counterpoint or perhaps a second countersubject in soprano; possibly another codetta
4. *Answer* given by bass in dominant key; countersubject in tenor; free counterpoint in the other voices

The exposition ordinarily ends when the last voice has completed the answer (or subject, as the case may be). Not all fugues have a regular countersubject, which deserves the name only if it is designed for subsequent use as a melodic accompaniment to the subject. If it is so used, it must be so constructed that it will sound well whether it is placed above, below, or between the other voices (invertible counterpoint).

After the exposition comes the development or modulatory section of the fugue, which ordinarily has two components: (1) the subject itself, which enters from time to time, frequently in other keys ("re-entries"), and (2) episodes which connect these recurring entries of the subject. Episodes fulfil two functions: they modulate to the keys in which the subject is to be presented; they may develop material derived from the subject or countersubject. Sequential repetition and dialogue between one voice and another are characteristic features of episodes.

The following are special devices by means of which thematic material may be imitated in polyphonic music. Do not expect to find many of these devices in many fugues.

Stretto—overlapping of subject and answer; a stretto may be complete, with all voices participating, or incomplete; the stretto is the most frequently used of these devices, probably because it has a cumulative, climactic effect

Imitation by inversion—imitation in contrary motion, ascending intervals being answered by descending ones and vice versa (not to be confused with harmonic inversion, the inversion of chords)

Imitation by augmentation—imitation involving the doubling of note values

Imitation by diminution—imitation involving the halving of note values

Imitation by retrograde movement—imitation in which a melodic line is either accompanied or answered by itself in reverse order, i.e., backward from the last note to the first

Imitation by contrary values—imitation in which the note values of a subject are altered while the melodic motion remains unchanged

A *double fugue* is a fugue with two subjects. One variety consists of a fugue on the first subject, one on the second subject, and a third on both subjects combined contrapuntally. The term is also used for an ordinary fugue in which the countersubject has considerable individuality and is combined consistently with the main subject throughout; in this kind of double fugue the subject and countersubject are exposed in two voices at the very beginning. There are also triple fugues; in fact, theoretically, there may be quadruple fugues, quintuple fugues, and so on.

The *canon* is the strictest species of imitation. All its voices have the same melody throughout, although starting at different points. The vertical lines of harmony and the horizontal lines of melody may be thought of as reinforced by diagonal lines marking the spacing of the imitation. Ingenious varieties of canon include the circle canon, where the melody leads back to the beginning and may be repeated several times (circle canons are sometimes called "rounds" or "catches"), and the spiral canon, where the melody ends a tone higher than it started and may thus be repeated up the scale until it reaches its starting point. The canon has been more largely a vocal type than an instrumental type.

Fugal procedure (less often, canonic procedure) is sometimes used within a section of a larger work. A passage in fugal style within a section (as in the development section of a work in sonata form) is called a *fugato*.

SINGLE TYPES

The names that have been applied—and still are applied—to separate pieces are legion. Few of them give any clue to the formal procedures which they will follow, although many, such as most names of dances, imply certain rhythmic (and, perhaps, melodic) characteristics, and some, such as a title like "Nocturne," are suggestive of an atmosphere or of a mood.

For example, *Invention* is a term obscure in meaning and rarely used but well known because of Bach's fifteen two-part "Inventions." Bach's fifteen three-part works of the same type he called "Sinfonias" (though modern editions title them "Inventions" also). His reasons in either case are not clear. It seems fair, however, to define "inventions" as studies in double or triple counterpoint, that is, invertible counterpoint in two or three voices.

Or take the term *Prelude*. This has an obvious literal meaning, borne out in names like "Prelude and Fugue" or "Prelude to Lohengrin," but it gives no clue whatsoever to the procedure. It has even been given to detached pieces such as the Preludes of Chopin, thereby losing what limited meaning it had.

Occasionally, names of formal procedures are used as titles of compositions, e.g., "Rondo," "Theme and Variations," "Fantasy," "Fugue," "Canon," and "Round."

Or a name may imply one procedure or another, depending upon who wrote it, when he wrote it, and where. For example, Lully, the composer of operas and ballets, developed in the late seventeenth century his famous *French overture*, an international type commencing with a slow, pompous introduction in dotted rhythm and proceeding to an allegro in imitative style on a short subject. This type of overture sometimes ended with a broad adagio passage, which was later extended to become a third movement, giving the pattern of slow-fast-slow for the whole. It became customary to perform the music of a series of the successful dance numbers from an opera or ballet as a suite apart from the opera itself and to introduce the suite with the overture of the opera. This practice led to the use of a French overture as the introductory movement of a suite of "modern dances" (composed not for opera or ballet but for the suite itself). It also led to the occasional practice of entitling the whole suite *Ouverture*. Around 1750, as the sonata and symphony became standard, the French overture disappeared. Meanwhile, another type of overture, the equally famous and international *Italian overture* had been developed by Alessandro Scarlatti from introductory pieces which he found labeled *Sinfonias*. It consisted of movements in the order allegro-adagio-allegro, all chiefly homophonic, and was an ancestor of the modern symphony. As the Italian overture began its metamorphosis into symphony and the French overture migrated also toward the category of a concert work, overtures which were actually overtures to operas became more closely connected with the opera itself through their employment of musical material from the opera, as in Rameau's "opera-overtures." Gluck, in the 1760's and 1770's, attempted to express the mood of the opening scene in the overture: instead of coming to a close before the curtain went up, it was made to run continuously into the scene. Mozart, Beethoven, and Weber used the overture to establish the emotional background of the whole action of the opera. They retained a set structure for it, derived from sonata form, however, whereas Wagner in his later operas returned to a practice suggested by Gluck and employed a *Vorspiel* ("Prelude") leading directly into the first scene. The Wagnerian Vorspiel is free in structure. Into its texture are woven many of the short, symbolic musical motives out of which the whole musical fabric of the opera is constructed. A very different kind of form was that of the nineteenth-century "grand opera" overture of France (as in Rossini, Auber, Meyerbeer, Thomas), which, like the overture of a modern musical comedy, was merely a potpourri of the most prominent melodies of the opera. Structurally the independent "concert-overture" of the nineteenth century followed the lead either of the full-structured Beethoven overture or of the Wagner Vorspiel.

Since we are about to be concerned with vocal types, it would be wise to list the traditional sources of Western vocal music.

1. *Plain song* ("Gregorian chant"), the sacred monophony in Catholic use since the early Middle Ages, is almost entirely of anonymous authorship. Its rhythm is non-metrical and not strongly accented.

2. *Traditional song* ("folk song"), the secular song found in all countries, preserved by oral tradition, and constantly replenished by new additions, is thought of as being entirely of anonymous authorship, though composers are sometimes known and even named when their songs are sung (e.g., Stephen Foster). Traditional song is metrical and usually highly formed.

3. The Protestant *hymn* (Lutheran *chorale* and Huguenot rhymed *psalm*) was begun during the Reformation by known composers, who used plain song, traditional song, motets and madrigals (see below), and their own invention, as sources. It is occasionally replenished by new additions. The chorale, especially, has an extraordinarily "square" (regular) rhythm, and all hymns are highly formal.

We now proceed to some vocal types. The *motet*, a choral type of Catholic liturgical music, is highly polyphonic and is usually sung "a cappella" (unaccompanied by instruments). It flourished in the sixteenth century, was kept rather artificially alive for a while in the seventeenth century, and is again prominent today, especially in France and England. Each voice is thought of as a melodic entity the quality of whose independence was emphasized in sixteenth-century publishing by issuing the music in separate part-books only, never in score. However, the voices must blend harmonically, and they are commonly otherwise interdependent in one of the following two ways:

1. They may be *rhythmically* alike—a passage in which all voices move together in the same rhythm is said to be in *familiar style*.

2. They may imitate one another in *melodic pattern*—a passage in which a melodic idea runs through two or more voices in succession is said to be in *imitative style*. Imitation is frequent in sixteenth-century usage.

Catholic sixteenth-century music is in spirit and style a polyphonic enlargement of plain song. To be sure, plain song is unmetrical, while the motet is metrical; but the latter preserves the smooth, almost accentless flowing rhythm of plain song. Indeed, a plain-song melody is often borrowed as material for polyphonic treatment (*cantus firmus*). Sometimes a traditional tune is similarly borrowed, in spite of the liturgical inappropriateness of its secular connotations.

The motet type is additive in form; that is, each phrase of the text has its own melodic setting. In any one section a repetition of ideas from another is seldom found. With every new section of the text, new musical material is introduced. In this additive form the number of sections in the music varies according to the number of sections in the text. More often than not the joints between the sections are smoothed over by allowing one voice to begin the new section while the others are completing the cadence of the old. This device is called *overlapping* of phrases.

The *madrigal* is the secular counterpart of the sixteenth-century motet and differs from it in the following respects: The melodic ideal is that of the traditional tune; the text is in the vernacular; the rhythm is more emphatic, often there are regularly recurring accented beats; chromaticism is fairly common, especially in the Italian school; repeated sections occur more frequently, the music may be quite formal in construction; refrains are common, mostly nonsense syllables, such as "fa-la-la."

The madrigal often treats the text programmatically, with such devices as a rising scale on the word "ascend," one voice singing unaccompanied on the word "alone," etc.—such effects are described by the term "madrigalesque."

The madrigal is chamber music: it is designed for one voice to each part. The singing of madrigals in the sixteenth and early seventeenth centuries was a social activity for amateur performers and was not meant primarily for listeners. This peculiarity was taken into account in the publishing of madrigals, which were made suitable for voices alone or for voices with instruments or for instruments alone, depending upon what was handy.

The madrigal composer used all types of short poems, from serious lyrics to doggerel verse. Poet and composer were often one and the same. The classifications of this kind of music are many, but let these broad designations suffice here: A madrigal is called a *chanson* in French; in German, it is called a *Lied;* the word "madrigal" itself is of Italian origin (*madrigale*).

Since Jacobean times the madrigal has been little cultivated. The energies of leading composers have gone elsewhere, with rare exceptions (in the works of Brahms, for example). Composers of smaller talent turned out a good many pieces of the type, which they called *glees* or, more generally, *part songs*, but these receive little attention from the cultivated public today. Many contemporary composers, however, have turned again more seriously to the madrigal. It is now a concert piece.

Chorale prelude is a name given to what are also called *organ chorales*. These were compositions based on a Protestant chorale and designed to be played just before the chorale was sung by the congregation. Like the fugue, the chorale prelude developed through the seventeenth century and culminated with Bach in the eighteenth. It may use the chorale melody as a cantus firmus, it may treat each phrase imitatively as in a motet, it may make a canon or fugue out of the first phrase, it may adopt the form of a set of variations or the free form of a fantasia, or it may merely ornament the melody or reproduce it in the upper voice, with counterpoint below.

The *solo song* is the sophisticated relative of the traditional tune. One often finds the two distinguished as *art song* and *folk song*.

The general type, which is very old, has changed little since the sixteenth century. Externally, the most marked change has been in the choice of favorite timbre for the instrumental accompaniment:

Sixteenth century: lute
Seventeenth and eighteenth centuries: harpsichord, perhaps with a cello reinforcing the bass, perhaps with flute or violin obbligato
Nineteenth and twentieth centuries: piano; for full-dress occasions, orchestra

The most usual names for the solo song are:

English: air (old sp., "ayre"), song, ballad
French: *chanson, mélodie*
Italian: *aria* (dim. *arietta*), *canzona* (dim., *canzonetta*), *romanza*
Spanish: *canción, cantiga*
German: *Lied*

Most song texts are stanzaic and lead naturally to a composition which repeats the same melody for each stanza. This kind of song is called *strophic*. In the nineteenth and twentieth centuries, another kind of song is almost as common as the strophic: a kind in which new sections of the text are always set to new music. There is no English word for this type; it is called by its German designation *durchkomponiert* ("through-composed"). Many songs are partly strophic, partly durchkomponiert. In the strophic song the composer may provide different accompaniments for the various stanzas. In general, much is made in song literature of the expressive value of the accompaniment.

The more dramatic a song is, the more it belongs in the concert room; the more traditionally lyrical, the more it belongs in the home as chamber music. One meets with the designations *concert song* and *scena* for the dramatic solo. The peculiarly personal nature of the lyric song is sometimes indicated even in countries other than Germany by the name *Lied*.

In the opera and oratorio, the prevalent form of aria is the "aria da capo," in which the basic musical instinct toward a ternary form is satisfied by the return of the whole first section after a middle section has been performed. This is what we should expect of a composition for orchestra; we would not find anything of this kind in a non-operatic theater. According to one established procedure, a broad, flowing aria da capo is followed by a "second movement," a rapid, brief, florid bravura piece. Usually, before a voice enters in the aria or ensemble, between sections, and at the end, the orchestra makes musical statements known as "ritornelli."

COMPOUND TYPES

Sometimes one finds a series of names, such as "fantasy and fugue," "recitative and aria" (often called, together, "scena"), and "Prelude, Chorale, and Fugue" (a piece by César Franck), which indicates some or all of the larger procedures or types involved. More often, a generic name is given to the whole piece.

The *suite* may be defined very simply as a work consisting of a number of movements, each in the character of a dance and all in the same key. Composers of the German classical suite of the eighteenth century, particularly Bach, were able to give a larger unity to what had before been merely a collection of pieces. With Bach a selection and order of movements was established which has come to be regarded as the standard, the norm—although it may be said to have been formulated simply in order that composers (including Bach himself) might deviate from it. This "norm" of the suite is easy to memorize: *A-C-S-O-G*, the letters standing for *allemande-courante-sarabande-optional-gigue*. A suite frequently begins with a *prelude*, however. Sometimes a suite movement is followed by a *double* (a variation). The dances from which the "optional" movement or group of movements was chosen were minuet, bourrée, gavotte, passepied, polonaise, rigaudon, anglaise, loure, and air (the last-named not a dance type, but a song type). By the time the regular members of the suite had been selected for inclusion, they had already lost their function as music for dancing and had become idealized types. The optional dances, however, which originated in the French ballets by Lully and others in the late seventeenth century, retained, even in the latest suites of Bach, their character as actual dance music. The form of most of the dances, of both varieties, is binary. In the simplest ones there are two strains, both repeated, each eight measures long, somewhat contrasted in style but not in rhythm, the first ending on the dominant. In more fully developed examples the second strain is two or three times longer than the first, approaching in its last portion something like a restatement of the first. Besides the late nineteenth-century orchestral suites comprising a selection of pieces from operas, ballets, or incidental music to plays, there has recently been a return to the writing of independent suites made up most characteristically of idealized folk-dance, folk-song, and modern-dance patterns not available to the eighteenth-century suite.

Type names which are scarcely more than variant terms for the eighteenth-century suite, though some of them represent hybrids of suite and sonata or symphony, include *cassation, divertimento, notturno, ordre, ouverture, partita,* and *serenade*.

The distinction between sonata and suite, in theory at least, is that the *sonata* is a compound work made up primarily of movements which are *not* dance types. Our procedure in discussing those most important types of the last two centuries, sonata, concerto, symphony, and associated species, will be to describe first the form which the types so named assumed most regularly during the last half of the eighteenth century and during the nineteenth century, from Haydn and Mozart to Brahms. The relation between these types and earlier types bearing the same names will then be very briefly traced.

Let us begin with some simple definitions.

A *sonata* is a composition of two, three, or four movements, written for piano or for another instrument, such as violin or cello, together with piano; it is absolute music, without program; in general, the movements are not derived from dance patterns; for each movement, however, certain forms are normal.

A *trio* is a sonata for three instruments. Most frequently a trio is for violin, cello, and piano. This variety may be called a "piano trio"; it is the kind usually meant when one says simply "trio." A "string trio" is for violin, viola, and cello.

A *quartet* is a sonata for four instruments. Unless there is qualification the term may be taken as synonymous with "string quartet," the instruments being two violins, viola, and cello. A "piano quartet" is for violin, viola, cello, and piano.

A *quintet* is a sonata for five instruments. A "piano quintet" is for string quartet plus piano, a "clarinet quintet" is for string quartet plus clarinet, a "viola quintet" is for string quartet plus an additional viola.

A *sextet* is a sonata for six instruments.

All the foregoing categories, except the piano sonata (and some persons would exclude the violin-and-piano or cello-and-piano sonata also) is *chamber music*, that is, music for a small group of instruments, each instrument playing a separate part.

A *symphony* is a sonata for full orchestra.

The normal scheme of movements of a sonata (using the term to include all the categories above) is Fast, Slow, Scherzo or Minuet, Fast. All but the third-movement terms are of course tempo indications. The terms "Scherzo" and "Minuet" describe the character of the third movement. This movement, at first a Minuet, was introduced into the sonata after the plan of a three-movement sonata Allegro-Adagio-Allegro had already been established. Sonatas, particularly those for one or two instruments, occasionally adhere to the three-movement plan. The substitution of Scherzo for Minuet became the norm in and after Beethoven. A slow Introduction often precedes the first Allegro, especially in symphonies.

The first movement proper (Allegro) of a sonata is normally in sonata form.

The reader must not confuse the term "sonata form," a one-movement form, with the type "sonata" as we are describing it here. The second movement (Adagio) is normally in ternary form or in sonata form; possibly, however, in binary form or variation form. The form of the third movement (Minuet or Scherzo) is described in connection with the discussion of the Mozart minuet earlier in this book. The last movement (Allegro, Presto) is normally in rondo form or sonata form, or sometimes in variation form.

The four movements of a symphony are likely to be considerably more extended than those of a chamber work, although some recent composers, interested above all in unity, yet disturbed by what they feel to be a mechanical aspect in recapitulation, have attempted to compress the symphony into the continuous flow of a single one-movement non-recapitulatory form. Some nineteenth-century composers attempted to combine program and symphony. This eventuated also in a one-movement form, the "symphonic poem," which will be discussed later.

The classical sonata and symphony avoided, in general, the use of thematic material from one movement in another movement, although subtle relationships can be felt. César Franck and his disciples, in the latter part of the nineteenth century, on the other hand, made it a principle that the form of the whole of a symphony and sonata should be "cyclic": that themes should be deliberately carried from one movement into the others.

A *concerto* is an exploitation of the contrast between a single instrument or a small group of instruments and the full orchestra. This definition covers both the seventeenth-and-eighteenth-century *concerto grosso*, in which two violins, a cello, and a harpsichord (or any other combination), known as the "concertino," alternate with the whole orchestra (the "tutti") in making a musical assertion, and the solo concerto ("violin concerto," for violin and orchestra; "piano concerto," for piano and orchestra), which belongs to the later historical period to which we have in general been restricting our definitions. The fast movements of concerti grossi are usually organized on the ritornello principle. The "tutti" begin by setting forth the *ritornello*. The rest of the movement may most readily be described as a discussion, in various related keys, of the ritornello by tutti and concertino, ending with a restatement, in whole or in part, of the ritornello.

In form, the first movement of the solo concerto is the offspring of a marriage between the sonata form and the ritornello. The orchestra begins with a ritornello which introduces part of the thematic material to be used. The solo instrument and orchestra then present the exposition, the end of which is continuous with a repetition by the orchestra of part of the ritornello. The development and recapitulation follow. The end of the recapitulation, again, is continuous with another repetition of part of the ritornello, with which the movement closes. If we compare the plan of a solo concerto with that of a sonata (including symphony, of course), we find that the concerto has usually but three movements, the Scherzo being omitted as inappropriate to concerto style; that the first movement of a concerto begins, not with an exposition (in two keys), but with a ritornello (all in the tonic key), which, nevertheless, is often called "the orchestra's exposition" because it contains a large part of the material later set forth in *the* exposition; that the last movement of a concerto is almost always a light and brilliant rondo; and that there is a *cadenza*, an improvisation interrupting and then effecting a cadence. Just before the end of the first movement— and perhaps of other movements—in the classical (late-eighteenth-century) concerto, the orchestra hung on to a second inversion of the tonic chord and then dropped out as the soloist launched into his cadenza, unaccompanied, on the themes of the movement. But presently the soloists took to writing their cadenzas out in advance rather than improvising them, and they tended to make them irrelevant displays of their virtuosity, weak musically. And so, in the mid-nineteenth century, composers themselves began to write the cadenza into the composition. Also, the cadenza moved from its position before the coda to a more climactic place between development and recapitulation, and the orchestral "exposition" frequently disappeared, the soloist embarking upon his own exposition at the very beginning. Concertos, more than symphonies, came to be conceived as a continuous flow of movements, without break, and the connection with the sonata plan has sometimes become remote. Contemporary composers, neoclassical in temperament and disgusted with the virtuoso character of the nineteenth-century solo concerto, have revived the concerto grosso.

Before taking leave of the post-1750 sonata plan, the reader should be warned that he may well never encounter a sonata which does not offer an exception to some assertion we have made.

Of the various services in Catholic usage the fundamental one is the *Mass*. The central part of the Mass is a literal (not merely symbolic) sacrifice which repeats the episode of the bread and wine at the Last Supper (see Matt. 26:26–28). The texts used are of two kinds, the Ordinary and the Proper.

The texts for the Ordinary are those which appear regularly in every Mass (with the exceptions noted later). The texts for the Proper are those which are "proper" either to a particular day of the church year (such as the Assumption of the Virgin, August 15) or to a special occasion with no prescribed date in the church calendar (such as the dedication of a church, or a Mass for the repose of a soul).

A musical setting of the entire Ordinary is called a "Mass." It is in effect, though not in name, a series of motets. The Ordinary alone is set, since the Proper changes from day to day, and a setting of both Ordinary and Proper would be good for only one day each year. An exception is the Mass for the Dead (*Requiem* Mass), which, since it has more widespread use, is a setting of both Ordinary and Proper. Individual sixteenth-century Masses are usually given names. Here are some examples:

Missa "Assumpta est Maria"—meaning that the Mass uses as cantus firmus a plain song whose text begins with the words quoted. This text, however, would not be used.

Missa "The Western Wynde"—the cantus firmus is an English traditional tune (secular) with that title. The words that go with the tune, however, would not be the original secular ones.

Missa "La sol fa re mi"—the cantus firmus is an often used arbitrary series of notes with certain pitch relationships (e.g., *D C B*-flat *G A*).

Missa sine nomine ("without a name")—the melodic material is original with the composer.

Liturgically, "Mass" refers to the entire service.

Musically, "Mass" refers to the musical setting of the Ordinary, except in the case of the "Requiem Mass," which includes the Proper.

A setting of any one text from the Proper is called a "motet" (in Anglican usage, an *anthem*). A motet has two titles, one indicating its liturgical function and another giving the first words of the text, for example:

Offertorium "Super Flumina"—the motet is to be used as an offertory; its text begins with the words quoted.

In liturgical order, the parts of the Mass open to choral treatment are named as follows:

ORDINARY	PROPER
	1. *Introit*—the first word of the introit in a Mass for the Dead is "Requiem"; hence the title "Requiem Mass"
2. *Kyrie*—a prayer for mercy; the only text which is in Greek, the others being in Latin	

ORDINARY

PROPER

3. *Gloria*—the "Canticle of Bethlehem," based on Luke 2:14—omitted during Advent and Lent, from the Requiem Mass, and from the Mass on ordinary week-days

4. Depending on the occasion, one or more of these: *Gradual, Alleluia, Sequence, Tract*

5. *Credo*—the Nicene Creed—omitted when there is no Gloria

6. *Offertory*

7. *Sanctus*—a hymn of praise, based on Isaiah 6:3 and Matt. 21:9—usually separated into two parts: *Sanctus* (Isaiah), *Benedictus* (Matthew)

8. *Agnus Dei*—based on John 1:29—is slightly changed for the Requiem

9. *Communion*

During the eighteenth and nineteenth centuries the Mass became more dramatic. Religious music was subjected to both operatic and instrumental influences. Musically, such works as the Requiem Masses of Mozart and Verdi, for instance, are oratorios.

Strictly defined, an *opera* is a drama which substitutes singing for speaking and is accompanied by an orchestra from beginning to end. There are important exceptions to this definition, but it offers us a clear distinction, at least, between an opera and a play with incidental music. The prime convention of opera is that of the sung text.

The general concept of opera before Wagner we shall label "number-opera"; the concept of and after Wagner we shall label "music-drama." Many of the finest operas in both the periods we are thus ticketing belie the labels. Generations of development and evolution are disregarded in so sweeping a classification. Nevertheless, the distinction is a useful one.

The action, the plot, in a number-opera is carried on through *recitative*, a type of vocal line which follows the inflections, cadences, and variations in pace of speech. Musically it is formless; its form is the form of spoken language, although it is sung. The orchestra restricts itself to providing chordal punctuation marks, or a reinforcement of accents. The recitative is periodically interrupted, however, by musical "numbers." The "numbers" include ballets, choruses, ensemble pieces for soloists and chorus, "concerted numbers" (duets, trios, quartets, quintets, sextets, sung by the main characters), and, most important and most frequent, solo *arias*. These numbers are so spaced amid the recitative and so arranged in relation to one another that, once we are familiar with the procedures of the number-opera, each species of number comes at just the right point to fulfil a pattern of expectation. The ensembles, for instance, customarily mark the ends of acts. During all numbers the action stops, the plot stands still. Even the speech fails to move forward; for lines and phrases, being completely subject to the musical pattern, are repeated, are succeeded by other lines, and are then repeated again. The singers of a duet tell each other the same thing over and over. Cadences occur regularly every sixteen bars, as one would expect of a musical pattern. Thought and action outside opera, however, do not move so regularly.

Wagner believed that the numbers framework was an altogether paralyzing convention. Only by discarding it entirely could musical and dramatic unity be achieved and integrated, he thought. The vocal ensemble is thrown out first of all, as one step further toward artifice even than the aria. Formal divisions into recitative and aria are broken down. In fact neither recitative nor aria, as a separate entity, exists. Whatever is dramatic and propulsive to the action in recitative or aria is assimilated into a single flow of melodic phrases, phrases which are not periodic, not regularly cadenced, not symmetrical, and do not repeat themselves. This flexible, free, continuous, half-declamatory melodic line is suited not only to an epic expansiveness but also to the reflection of momentary impulses of lyric feeling which defy set patterns. That this kind of melodic line is slower even than recitative (plus time-out for aria) did not bother Wagner. He was not interested in realism per se. The real action is the inner action—the feelings. The home of the inner action is the orchestra. The vocal element is to be thought of not in terms of solo with accompaniment but rather as a part, not the most important part either, of the orchestration. The orchestra music, like the vocal line, is continuous. The vocal line, however, must of necessity break off and pick up when the dialogue breaks off and picks up, whereas the orchestral flow is sustained from the beginning of the prelude to the end of an act. It can be made continuous in this fashion through the avoidance of perfect cadences, through constant modulation, and through the polyphonic character of its structural fabric. This fabric is woven with threads of recurrent short motives, each susceptible to modification in accord with change in situation or feeling. These motives and their manipulation take on symbolic meanings.

Here, then, is a part of the theory, and practice, of Wagner. Some of it was anticipated by Gluck a hundred years before. Many of the details have been rejected by composers who have written opera since Wagner. There is a mistiness about some of his ideas which has been distasteful to many composers. And yet the basic principles of his music-drama rather than those of the number-opera have been the rule since his day (a quite recent return of neoclassical composers to the number-opera may be taken, for the present at least, as merely the exception). Even in the "realistic" operas of composers who have reacted against the windy symbolism of Wagner, the orchestra is always as important as the singers, or more important than they, and it busies itself from the beginning to the end of the work with a continuous symphonic depiction of the action and commentary thereon. The modern aria seems to grow out of and to be a part of this sustained flow of sound. Wagner's system of motives has been thought by many composers to be too mechanical, but they have nevertheless taken the hint from him and have achieved unity and an increased poignancy through the employment of recurrent characterizing phrases.

Certain other historical distinctions among kinds of opera may be disposed of briefly. An obvious difference is that between the Italian *opera seria* (serious opera) and *opera buffa* (comic or jocose opera, which grew out of short *intermezzi* performed between the acts of serious opera). Besides humor, comic opera introduced a richness of characterization which serious opera lacked. The distinction between the French *opéra comique* and other opera is less obvious. The definition is sharp enough: *opéra comique* is opera which contains spoken dialogue as well as sung. *Opéra comique* is therefore an exception to our initial definition of opera as a form in which the dialogue is sung throughout. Moreover, *opéra comique* is by no means always comic—Bizet's *Carmen* is a famous example of *opéra comique* which is tragic (the original version of Carmen included spoken dialogue). In general, from *opéra comique* in France there has developed an opera more lyric and more popular in character than "grand opera," regardless of whether or not there is spoken dialogue and regardless of whether the plot is comic or serious.

The opera, ever since its beginnings in the early seventeenth century, has strongly influenced all other types of music. We are here concerned with the manifestations of the operatic spirit in vocal music which is not performed as drama but is nevertheless permeated by the dramatic.

The opera before Wagner has the following musical components: overture, recitatives, arias, ensemble numbers (duets, trios, etc.), dances, and choruses. Orchestral accompaniment is universal. Now take all these components, even perhaps the dances, and transfer them bodily to a musical setting of any text with dramatic implications, whether it be the story of Christ's crucifixion, Milton's "Samson Agonistes," the Requiem Mass, or what not. You will have something called variously an *oratorio*, a *cantata*, a *Mass*, or a *Passion*. Allow a song to take on the accents of an operatic aria, and you will have a dramatic "concert song." Give a text suitable for treatment in a madrigal a setting full of strong expression and sudden contrasts, and you will have something quite like a chorus from an opera. This is only a slight indication of the extent to which the opera has altered the face of music. Its influence is everywhere, in instrumental and vocal music, sacred and secular.

An *oratorio* is in effect an unstaged opera. The lack of stage action necessitates such phrases as "And then he said," but there is always action to the mind's eye. The text may be either sacred or secular but is more often sacred, probably because religious literature abounds in subjects of unsurpassed dramatic power, and yet the public taste in many countries frowns on the representation of sacred persons on the stage. The dramatic oratorio eliminates the dilemma.

A *Passion* is an oratorio whose subject is the events of the last week in the life of Christ. In the works of the German Protestant composers the biblical story is often interlarded with and interpreted by devotional lyrics set to the music of the Lutheran chorales. These chorale tunes are then treated polyphonically with a kind of Protestant counterpart of the Catholic cantus firmus technique. A Passion is further identified by the name of the particular evangelist from whose gospel the text is derived, for example, Bach's "Passion According to St. Matthew."

The word *cantata* has two meanings:

A *choral cantata* is a short oratorio, usually handling a somewhat less dramatic subject than is used for the oratorio proper. Relative shortness, however, is more characteristic of the type than is relative dramatic quality. The subject may be either sacred or secular. In the most famous of all sacred cantatas, those of J. S. Bach, the same effective use of chorales is found as was mentioned above in connection with the Passion.

A *chamber cantata* (*solo cantata* or *duet cantata*) is a species of chamber music especially popular in the seventeenth and eighteenth centuries. It is almost always secular. The subject is usually unhappy love in the artificially pastoral setting of which poets of the time were extremely fond. A chamber cantata is a series of recitatives and arias (with perhaps some duets), corresponding exactly to a short operatic scene, except for the smallness of the accompanying instrumental forces (often only a harpsichord). The French and Italian composers excelled in the chamber cantata.

EXTRA-MUSICAL CONSIDERATIONS

When music is used as a background for something else, as in "mood music" for radio plays and for films, the extra-musical factors tend to be the organizing force, and the listener's attention is strongly drawn to the music only when the composer has been unsuccessful in making it an unobtrusive support. In a successful ballet, music is so illuminated by the dance, and vice versa, because of the strong compatibility of these two more abstract arts, that peculiarities of musical procedure are unlikely to arise. But there is one kind of music, *program music*, intended to stand by itself with the aid of literary foreknowledge on the part of the audience, which has given rise to problems of procedure. In general, however, composers of program music have relied heavily on the well-known procedures and typical movements of absolute music; some (Strauss, for example) have gone so far as to express the hope that their pieces would stand by themselves as music without knowledge of the program.

The *symphonic poem*, or tone poem, was invented in the very middle of the nineteenth century. In spite of the richness of substance and the technical expertness of Berlioz' programed symphonies, the compound four-movement symphonic form proved recalcitrant as a vehicle for communication of a program. Stories or poems or emotional experiences do not naturally arrange themselves in allegro-adagio-scherzo-vivace sequences. To retain the program of the programmatic symphony and something of the largeness of the symphonic concept, yet not to be thwarted by unmalleability of form, Liszt inaugurated the symphonic poem, a single, one-movement programmatic type. Usually the form of the whole was a free adaptation of the first-movement form of a symphony. Themes were transformed and presented in new disguises rather than developed. Symphonic poems have tended to be poetic in character, at first full of literary associations, later more purely descriptive. There has been a pronounced nationalism. Richard Strauss enlarged the scope of the program, pushing it both toward the realistic and toward the grandiosely philosophical.

8. SCALES

How have the various scales used in our music been chosen? This question has never been satisfactorily answered, because any answer lies almost entirely in the realm of speculation. Various rationalizations of these scales, however, are known and recorded. The most recent rationalizations are based upon the harmonic series.

Since the harmonic series is firmly imbedded in the very nature of tone, it would seem to provide a natural basis for building scales. Essentially, a scale involves a division of the octave into intervals.

To construct a diatonic scale of *just intonation*, as it is called, we shall select from the harmonic series certain intervals formed by different pairs of harmonics. If the reader will refer to the diagram of the harmonic series, he will find that the first and second harmonics are an octave apart and that their frequency ratio is 2:1; that the second and third harmonics are a fifth apart and their frequency ratio 3:2; that the third and fourth harmonics are a fourth apart and their frequency ratio 4:3. Similarly, the ratio of a major third is 5:4, of a major sixth, 5:3, of a major second, 9:8, and of a major seventh, 15:8. These intervals and their corresponding frequency ratios are here listed in an order such that the higher notes of the intervals taken in succession form an ascending scale in the major mode.

Interval	Frequency Ratio
Prime (unison)	1:1
Major second	9:8
Major third	5:4
Perfect fourth	4:3
Perfect fifth	3:2
Major sixth	5:3
Major seventh	15:8
Octave	2:1

The seventh, eleventh, thirteenth, and fourteenth harmonics (in brackets in the diagram) are not used in rationalizing intervals because they are not in tune with any of our scales and their pitches can be only approximately represented on the staff. Since a frequency ratio expresses a relation between two tones, the actual pitch of either is irrelevant. Two notes forming a perfect fifth have frequencies that stand in the relation of 3 to 2 no matter where they are located in the musical range. We can therefore arbitrarily set the A above middle C as the first note of our scale and calculate all intervals from it. If the frequency of A is 440 vibrations per second, then that of B, which forms the interval of a major second with A, will be $\frac{9}{8} \times 440$, or 495 vibrations per second; the frequency of C-sharp, which forms the interval of a major third with A, will be $\frac{5}{4} \times 440$, or 550 vibrations per second; and so on for the other degrees of the scale.

A scale so based on the natural harmonics with acoustically correct intervals would seem to be a perfect scale, but actually its use is very limited, because a piece of music written in the last few centuries seldom confines itself to a single scale. Suppose, for instance, that a piece starting out in the scale just introduced should change to a similar scale constructed on the note B—in other words, suppose it should modulate. We would get a new frequency for the note C-sharp:

As the *third* note of the *A* scale, *C*-sharp has a lower frequency than it does as the *second* note of the *B* scale. This is only one instance of many such discrepancies. Music based on the "just" diatonic scale must limit itself to the rather narrow confines of this one scale if it is to sound in tune; it cannot modulate to other keys. There are three possible solutions to this difficulty. One is to provide several *A*'s, *B*'s, *C*-sharps, etc. This would probably require some 70 or 80 notes to the octave—an impractical solution, especially for keyboard instruments. The *meantone system*, used widely in the past, effected a compromise by making a limited number of related keys fairly accurate in their tuning, the others being badly out of tune. The present system of *equal temperament* divides the octave into 12 equal intervals and so distributes its acoustical inaccuracies evenly over the whole scale.[1] This tempered tuning makes it possible to change from a scale based on one tone to a scale based on another—to another "key"; all are alike available, all are alike to some degree impure. Equal temperament is possible only because tones have a certain "breadth"; the ear either does not detect slight differences in frequency or, if it does, easily adjusts to them. The tempered tuning of the *A* scale given here should be compared with the scale of just intonation.

A comparison between these frequencies and those of just intonation shows that the octave is the same; the second, fourth, and fifth differ only slightly; while the other intervals diverge more widely. The tempered scale, then, approximates the mathematical simplicity of the scale of just intonation, and its intervals (save the octave, which remains the same) conform closely but not exactly to those of the harmonic series.

1. The frequency ratio of the octave is 2:1; that is, the frequency of any note is twice that of the note an octave below it bearing the same letter name. To fill in the octave interval with 12 semitones, it is necessary to find the factor which, when multiplied by itself 12 times, will equal 2. This factor is the twelfth root of 2, or 1.05946. The successive powers of this number give the relative frequencies of the tones of the chromatic scale.

One might ask why acoustical "purity" has been considered desirable. The reason lies in the difference tones. Any two tones sounding together give rise to a third tone whose frequency is the difference between the frequencies of the first two. Now if, for instance, one takes a major triad in just intonation (and a glance at the diagram of the harmonic series will show this), the difference tones arising from the various intervals will all either coincide with tones already present or reproduce them in other octaves. This makes for a "smooth" sound.

However, the art of music has not restricted itself to the use, in any one piece, of major triads only, in one key only. Tempered tuning is apparently here to stay.

KINDS OF SCALES

A great many scale patterns are possible. Some of the more widely used scales are:

1. *Diatonic*, consisting of 7 tones, using both whole-steps and half-steps. One kind of diatonic scale would be:

2. *Chromatic*, consisting of 12 semitones (half-steps):

3. *Whole-tone*, consisting of 6 whole-tones (whole-steps):

4. *Pentatonic*, consisting of 5 tones within the octave, the five arranged in any one of a variety of ways. The one arrangement most widely known is this, which contains no semitones:

(This scale can be obtained also by playing only the black keys on the piano.)

MODES OTHER THAN MAJOR AND MINOR

Ecclesiastical modes (church modes, medieval modes), the modes of the diatonic scale used in Gregorian chant, in medieval and Renaissance art music, and
in much folk music, differ from one another in the arrangement of semitones
and whole-tones within each tetrachord. The most common ecclesiastical
modes are:

Older names for the modes familiar to us as "major" and "minor" are, respectively, "Ionian" and "Aeolian."

MUSICAL SUPPLEMENT

MUSICAL SUPPLEMENT

Themes from Longer Works:

MOZART: QUARTET IN G MAJOR, K.387, MINUET

137

CHOPIN: PRELUDE NO. 6

BEETHOVEN: PIANO SONATA, OP. 2, NO. 3
slow movement

144

BACH: FUGUE IN C MINOR FROM THE *WELL-TEMPERED CLAVIER*, BOOK I

FUGA II.

J. S. BACH

Note: Bach's *Well-Tempered Clavier* is a set of forty-eight preludes and fugues in all the major and minor keys.

1. ADESTE FIDELES

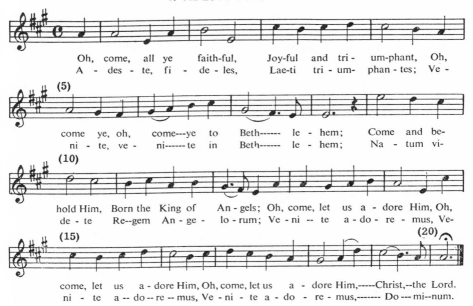

Oh, come, all ye faith-ful, Joy-ful and tri - um-phant, Oh,
A - des - te, fi - de - les, Lae-ti tri - um - phan - tes; Ve -

(5)

come ye, oh, come---ye to Beth------ le - hem; Come and be-
ni - te, ve - ni------te in Beth------ le - hem; Na - tum vi-

(10)

hold Him, Born the King of An - gels; Oh, come, let us a - dore Him, Oh,
de - te Re--gem An - ge - lo - rum; Ve - ni -- te a - do - re - mus, Ve-

(15) **(20)**

come, let us a - dore Him, Oh, come, let us a - dore Him,-----Christ,--the Lord.
ni - te a -- do -- re -- mus, Ve - ni - te a - do - re - mus,------- Do --- mi--num.

2. THE LITTLE SHIP

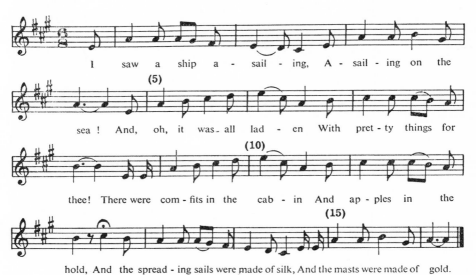

I saw a ship a - sail - ing, A - sail - ing on the

(5)

sea ! And, oh, it was all lad - en With pret - ty things for

(10)

thee! There were com - fits in the cab - in And ap - ples in the

(15)

hold, And the spread - ing sails were made of silk, And the masts were made of gold.

147

3. AU CLAIR DE LA LUNE

Au claire de la lu-ne, Mon a-mi Pier-rot, Pre-te-moi ta

plu-me Pour e-crire un mot. Ma chandelle est mor-te,

Je n'ai pas de feu; Ou-vre-moi ta por-te Pour l'amour de Dieu.

4. ALL THROUGH THE NIGHT

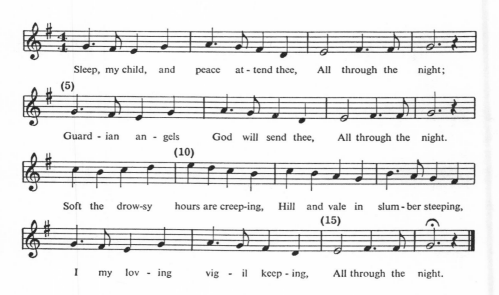

Sleep, my child, and peace at-tend thee, All through the night;

Guard-ian an-gels God will send thee, All through the night.

Soft the drow-sy hours are creep-ing, Hill and vale in slum-ber steeping,

I my lov-ing vig-il keep-ing, All through the night.

5. WHEN JOHNNY COMES MARCHING HOME

When John - ny comes marching home a - gain, Hur - rah! Hur-

rah! We'll give him a heart - y welcome then, Hur - rah! Hur-

rah! The men will cheer-- the boys will shout, The la - dies they -- will

all turn out, And we'll all feel gay When John - ny comes marching home!

6. WHAT CHILD IS THIS?

What Child is this who, laid to rest, On Ma - ry's lap is sleep-ing? Whom

an - gels greet with an - thems sweet, While shep - herds watch are keep-ing?

This, this is Christ the King, Whom shep-herds guard, and an - gels sing:

Haste, haste to bring Him laud, The Babe, the Son of Ma -- ry.

7. FAIREST LORD JESUS

Fair-est Lord Je --- sus, King of all na -- ture, Oh; thou of

God and man the son! Thee will I cher -- ish,

Thee will I hon -- or, Thou, my soul's glo-ry, joy, and crown.

8. JESUS, MEINE ZUVERSICHT

Je - sus, mein - e Zu - ver-sicht und mein Heiland ist im Leb-en:
Die - ses weiss ich, soll ich nicht da - rum mich zu - frieden geb-en?

Was die lan - ge Tod - es - nacht mir auch fur Ge - dank - en macht.

9. FLOW GENTLY, SWEET AFTON

Flow gen-tly, sweet Af-ton, a-mong thy green braes; Flow gently, I'll

sing thee a song in thy praise; My Ma-ry's a--sleep by thy

mur-mur-ing stream; Flow gently, sweet Af-ton, dis-turb not her dream. Thou

stock-dove whose echo re-sounds from the hill, Ye wild whistling

black-birds in yon thorn-y dell, Thou green-crest-ed lap-wing, thy

scream-ing for-bear; I charge you, dis-turb not my slum-ber-ing fair.

10. BRING A TORCH, JEANNETTE, ISABELLA!

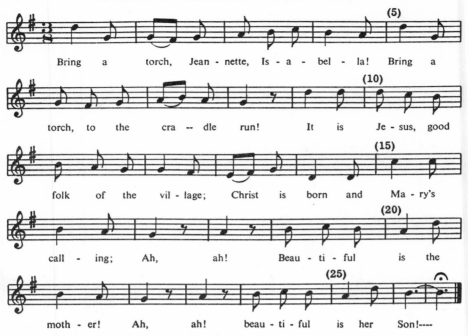

Bring a torch, Jean - nette, Is - a - bel - la! Bring a torch, to the cra -- dle run! It is Je - sus, good folk of the vil - lage; Christ is born and Ma - ry's call - ing; Ah, ah! Beau - ti - ful is the moth - er! Ah, ah! beau - ti - ful is her Son!----

11. EARLY ONE MORNING

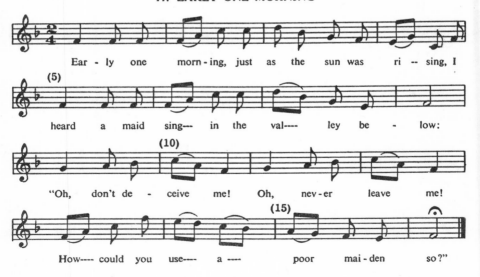

Ear - ly one morn - ing, just as the sun was ri -- sing, I heard a maid sing--- in the val---- ley be - low: "Oh, don't de - ceive me! Oh, nev - er leave me! How---- could you use---- a ---- poor mai - den so?"

12. TWO TRADITIONAL TUNES

13. THEME FROM *PIANO SONATA IN A MAJOR*, MOZART

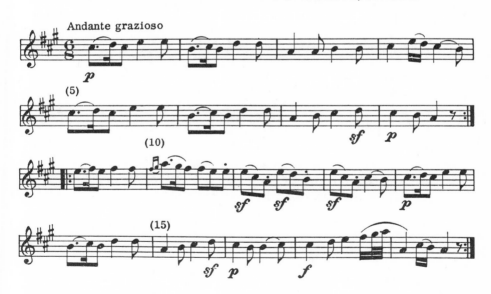

14. THEME FROM *JUPITER SYMPHONY*, MOZART

15. THEME FROM *CAPRICCIO ESPAGNOL*, RIMSKY-KORSAKOV

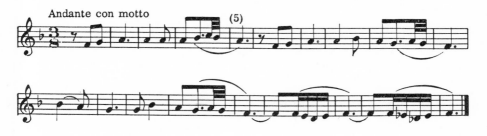

16. HAYDN'S THEME USED BY BRAHMS

GLOSSARY-INDEX

This glossary-index is selective, having been put together primarily for these three purposes:

1. To help in following scores which use foreign words. Intentional omissions have been made here wherever possible. For example, the reader probably does not need to be told that in a German score "Klarinette" stands for "clarinet."

2. To act more as a vocabulary for the book than as an index to it. For example, the word "phrase" is used far oftener in the text than the index might imply.

3. To guide the reader who has found the trees but missed the forest. The entries under "continuity," "expectation," and "rhythm" have been especially designed for this purpose.

The following abbreviations are used:

F, French
G, German
I, Italian

not., notation
vs, versus
s, summary at the end of chapter 6

8 va ,19	※ , 15	°, 24	$\dot{\mathfrak{f}}$, 24
8 va bassa, 19	♭, 15	+, 24	{, 22
⌒, 8	♭♭, 15	:‖, 22	⌒, 24
♯, 14	♮, 20	‖: :‖, 22	⦚, 22

A, 14
AA', binary, 54
a2, a3, etc.: winds, doubled, trebled, etc., 80; strings, divided into two parts, three parts, etc.
ABA, ternary, 32, 34, 68, 103
absolute music, 115
a cappella, 110
accelerando, 11
accent (rhythm), 26, 27, 29
adagio, 10
additive form, 97, 106, 111
"Adeste Fideles," 27–31, 37, 40, 42, 54, 147
Aeolian mode, 128
Agnus dei, 119
air, 113

Ais (G), *A*♯
allegretto, 10
allegro, 10
Alleluia, 119
allemande, 114
Althoboe (G), English horn
alto: female voice of low range; in four-voiced texture, second voice from top
alto clef, 19
amen cadence, 51
amplitude (of tone), 3
andante, 10
andantino, 10
anglaise, 114
answer, 62, 66, 107

157